M000215605

SONGS
BEFORE
DAWN

A Collection of Traditional Love Poems

Adonna Marie Gipe

abbott press

Copyright © 2017 Adonna Marie Gipe.

All rights reserved. No part of this book may be used or reproduced by any means,
graphic, electronic, or mechanical, including photocopying, recording, taping or by
any information storage retrieval system without the written permission of the author
except in the case of brief quotations embodied in critical articles and reviews.

Scriptures taken from the Holy Bible, New International Version®, NIV®.
Copyright © 1973, 1978, 1984, 2011 by Biblica, Inc.™ Used by permission
of Zondervan. All rights reserved worldwide. www.zondervan.com The
"NIV" and "New International Version" are trademarks registered in
the United States Patent and Trademark Office by Biblica, Inc.™

Abbott Press books may be ordered through booksellers or by contacting:

Abbott Press
1663 Liberty Drive
Bloomington, IN 47403
www.abbottpress.com
Phone: 1 (866) 697-5310

Because of the dynamic nature of the Internet, any web addresses or links contained in
this book may have changed since publication and may no longer be valid. The views
expressed in this work are solely those of the author and do not necessarily reflect the
views of the publisher, and the publisher hereby disclaims any responsibility for them.

Any people depicted in stock imagery provided by Thinkstock are models,
and such images are being used for illustrative purposes only.
Certain stock imagery © Thinkstock.

ISBN: 978-1-4582-2134-6 (sc)
ISBN: 978-1-4582-2135-3 (e)

Library of Congress Control Number: 2017914026

Print information available on the last page.

Abbott Press rev. date: 11/07/2017

My heart is steadfast, O God;
I will sing and make music with all my soul.
Awake, harp and lyre!
I will awaken the dawn.
I will praise you, O Lord, among the nations;
I will sing of you among the peoples.
Psalm 108:1-3 ~NIV

To my beloved friend, Lin Gilliland,

who gently pushed until I published my poetry.

I think she would like this book.

Contents

Dr. James L. Bond served as president of Point Loma Nazarene University for fourteen years, until elected to the position of General Superintendent in the Church of the Nazarene. He has also served on both state and national boards of education.

After receiving his BA from Pasadena College, (now Point Loma University) he was drafted by the Lakers to play professional basketball, but declined in order to continue his education at Nazarene Theological Seminary where he earned a Master of Divinity. He later earned the Doctor of Ministry from Fuller Theological Seminary.

Dr. Bond is also the recipient of three honorary doctorates from Southern Nazarene University, Northern Arizona University and Point Loma Nazarene University.

He and his wife Sally (Whitcanack,) have two married children and nine grandchildren.

Foreword

Adonna Gipe and her husband Bob, have been cherished friends of mine and my wife Sally's since college days. Adonna wrote regularly for the college paper and continued to pursue this writing interest throughout her life. She has taught creative writing to middle and senior high school students, has published in numerous magazines, and won many prizes in national contests.

I have known much of this history, but only recently read most of the material contained in this book. The volume and quality of her work are outstanding! Each piece, and the body collectively, reflect the truth of the old adage – "The years teach."

Adonna demonstrates exceptional giftedness for writing as an art form. *Words* – how amazing when arranged so adroitly, creatively and exquisitely! Thoughtful reading of this poetry can ignite passion, send a spirit soaring, call one back to authentic family, moral and spiritual values and even warm a dampened spirit. To read these remarkable works with perception is to enter a wonderland of provocative and inspirational insight. I heartily endorse this body of poetry written by one who has blessed us with a grace-filled life and now with her scintillating pen.

Jim L. Bond

Preface

These poems were not written to fill a book, but were simply the outpouring of a creative spirit over a lifetime of writing.

My mother often recited poetry to my sisters and me while we played in her kitchen as children. When I learned to read, I found I enjoyed reading the words in the hymnbooks she kept in her piano bench, and one day, to my delight, I discovered, tucked away in an old dresser in the attic, a copy of the book, <u>101 Favorite Poems</u>. Every night thereafter, I poured over its pages until sleep interrupted. So, perhaps it's no surprise my poetry tends to follow a more traditional style.

My sisters and I were blessed to have, along with our poetically inclined mother, a creative father who encouraged his children to read books and to speak and write proper English. Unquestionably, both parents contributed to my love of words.

When I was eight, I wrote my first poem in the form of a letter to Santa, and my teacher liked it enough to post it on a bulletin board in the hallway. Many more poems followed. Around this same time, our pastor, Rev. William Booth-Clibborn, author of several books and a published poet, took a kindly interest. He was a frequent guest at our dinner table, and long before my birth, had written the words to what has become a popular Christian song, "Down from His Glory." During his visits to our home, he would ask if I had any new poems to show him. He generously offered solid suggestions and positive reinforcement, and to a budding writer, the impact was incalculable.

I can't explain the creative urge which makes some children want to paint pictures, some to sing and some to write, but it is a common urge and most have felt it in some form. My three sisters, Virginia, Audrey and Shirley, seemed to enjoy my writing as much as I enjoyed their music. They eventually insisted I gather some poems into a book they could hold in their hands. The result is this collection.

In college and beyond, I was blessed to encounter many outstanding teachers who influenced and encouraged me. Three who stand out are Susan Rushton, Bud Gardner and Ray Griffin. They taught me to trust the creative process, to dare to be original, and to revise and polish until the beauty shone. My gratitude to each of them runs deep.

If possible, I would list the many students who filled my classrooms and taught me more than I ever anticipated, but I hope they will know how much I enjoyed and appreciated them. Their names and faces are forever in my heart.

Without the unwavering love and inspiration of my lifelong friend and husband, Bob Gipe, I doubt this would have been completed, but he knows how grateful I am.

Last, but always first, is my gracious God, from whom comes every good and perfect gift and who never ceases to inspire and delight both heart and mind. It is my deepest desire to honor Him in all I do.

Adonna Gipe
Auburn, California
July, 2017

Songs Before Dawn

I awake before the dawn is breaking,
all my quiet dreams forsaking,
to watch the regal sun rise from its throne

and spread its velvet robes of crimson
softly over earth's horizon ...
the most amazing sight my eyes have known.

High in the sky the stars wink down,
as heaven folds her sequined gown
and stores it out of sight. The rising dawn,

majestic in its radiant light,
dismisses merrily the night;
the dark and all its solemn stillness, gone.

As deer rise from their beds nearby,
wild geese flee hovered clouds to cry
their glee across the meadow, bright with dew.

My heart, in waking ecstasy,
discerns life's pulsing poetry
and sings afresh new love songs... just for You.

Tread Lightly

Tread lightly as you go
exploring in this strange terrain, my heart.
Tread lightly now, and slow,
and watch for there is much you do not know.

Speak softly, as in prayer,
for in a sense it is a hallowed part.
Speak gently and take care,
for all my sacred self is sheltered there.

Look kindly, if you would,
and shun the shadowed places, and the rough.
Look lovingly for good
and linger if you like, where few have stood.

Wait patiently for me,
and when I know the way is warm enough,
I'll come and yield the key,
and with your hand in mine, we'll wander free.

The Sunlit Strand

There is a place where love walks hand in hand
with poetry and melodies of song.
It is a sunlit stretch of golden sand
where only gentle hearts in love belong.

The sliding breakers stroke the silken shore
with nature's quiet rhythm, as the tide
comes with a sigh, then slips away once more ...
a place where peace and beauty both reside.

One day I walked along this golden strand
and touched a rainbow in the circling mist.
A sudden wave of love I'd never planned
washed over me ... I knew I had been kissed

by heaven's sweetest blessing, rare but real
and ever since that day beside love's sea,
I've marveled at the happiness I feel,
and try to tell it in my poetry.

Old Leaves and Warm Words

Old leaves stir and turn
in the morning breeze,
scuffing along the walk
like reluctant children.

I listen to their distant whispers
and hear your words,
soft and far away,
promising me a prayer.

I try to hear the poetry
the leaves speak,
but they scatter out of reach.

Your words though,
beam like sunlight through the trees,
touching me with warmth.

You Left the Door Ajar

Your heart was there for all the world to see,
for love stepped out and left the door ajar.
I, passing by, found some was meant for me,
and wandered in to sit beside your hearth.

The crackling fire of laughter warmed my soul,
as every word you spoke sent smiles of light
to chase away the shadows, fill the hole
old sorrow left, the remnants of my night.

Now every morning, with the door swung wide,
the sun streams in and all small creatures too.
None need be cold ... none need be shut outside,
for all are welcome to abide with you

and share the space inside your giant heart,
where warmth and laughter reign and love is free ...
where grace and peace adorn the walls like art
and every window shines with poetry.

Perhaps

If I could tell you what you mean to me …
if only you might sense how like the sea,
my love, in boundless waves, flows endlessly,
perhaps you'd know my heart.

If I could give you every gift on earth,
and thereby help you see how much you're worth …
if I could fill your days with fun and mirth,
perhaps you'd know my heart.

If I could light the stars that fill your eyes,
and give you golden wings to sail the skies,
or cause your dreams to all be realized,
perhaps you'd know my heart.

But I have neither words nor ways to say
how deep, how strong the love I send your way;
and yet I cling to this one hope … someday
perhaps you'll know my heart.

I Thought I'd Try

I thought I'd carve a poem on a tree
to say how much your love has meant to me,
but nowhere could be found
one big enough around
to hold the whole of all my poetry!

I thought I'd spin a cobweb from a star
to tell the world how wonderful you are,
but light years filled with lace
could never quite replace
the width and depth of love within my heart.

I thought I'd fill the oceans with my love,
for all your gifts, I am unworthy of.
But endless waves cascading
and countless gulls parading,
cannot begin to tell the half thereof.

I wish that I could whisper, without tears,
how precious to my eyes your face appears,
but there's no way to show
how blessed I am to know
such unrelenting love throughout the years!

Showers of Love

The day is stormy, but my heart breathes joy.
The wind sings sweetly through the swaying trees,
as fields stretch wide, like lengths of corduroy,
their sprouting crops uplifting thirsty leaves.

The ceaseless rain reminds me of your love,
the love outpoured so freely from your heart.
The sun might hide behind the clouds above ...
a chill may linger when we are apart,

but rain paints every tree with budding green
and causes blooms to burst from tulip fronds.
The meadow grass is washed, each blade rinsed clean,
as frogs splash happily in nearby ponds.

I hear the drumming of your heart in mine
and know the dreary day holds far less gloom
because you've come my way. By God's design,
the showers of your love make my life bloom.

Fragrant Memories

The rain brings fragrant memories
of distant days from long ago.
Like drops of moisture in the seas,
they glitter as they splash below.

As I surrender to my dreams,
the rain brings fragrant memories.
Beneath the clouds a small light gleams
and flickers in the wisp of breeze.

Perhaps a ship out on the seas
is searching for a path to shore.
The rain brings fragrant memories
of simpler days I've lived before.

I sip from evening's tinted glass
as shadows wrap the sighing trees,
and marvel how the decades pass.
The rain brings fragrant memories.

Love Lights My Way

I was a sailboat, tossed about,
lost on a stormy sea,
but you were the lighthouse on the shore
which lovingly rescued me.

I was a storm cloud dark with doubt
adrift in a sky of gray,
but you were the sun whose warming light
drove all of my darkness away.

I was the waves in a raging sea
dashing the trembling sand,
but you were the calm in the changing tide,
as you tenderly took command.

You are my light, my warmth, my strength;
you are the love of my heart.
No longer adrift or lost, I've found
my port, and will never depart.

Only God

A long, long time ago, when Earth was young
and waterfalls and oceans flowed at will,
a star was born and in the heavens, hung
above the marble planet, cold and still.

For years unknown, its light traversed the dark
before it entered our eyes' grateful view.
And so it is, this love which fills my heart,
has somehow found its way, through time, to you.

Whose hand was this, who placed the star up there
and made its radiance shine with gentle light?
Whose mind conceived such beauty to be shared
for centuries to come, through lilac night?

And Who, with kind compassion unexplained,
allowed this love, which had no place to go,
to find you in the night? It's God-ordained,
for only His great plan could make it so.

In Lieu of Words

To write a poem filled with heartfelt love,
to make it sing with all the music of
the hemisphere, and know my words reveal
the depth and power of this love I feel,
is more than I could ever hope or ask.

To sing in purest tones my gratitude,
and have both melody and words exude
the essence of my joy in knowing you,
would seem the very least that I could do,
and yet it is, for me, a hopeless task.

In lieu of words or melodies of song,
I pray I might display, my whole life long,
how deeply flows this river of devotion,
to fill the surging sea of pure emotion.
May you, in love's warm sun, forever bask.

Singing Strings

I vowed I would not love him.
My heart could not be swayed.
"I'm strong," I said. "I'll keep my head.
This fiddle can't be played."

He claimed it didn't matter;
his love would wait for me.
I had my pride, but couldn't hide
from love's pure melody.

At last, in full surrender,
my silent heart gave in ...
and now I know, with love's strong bow,
he plays this violin.

I Wish I Had a Song to Sing

I wish I had a song to sing,
a song you'd love to hear.
I'd sing it in the softest voice,
a voice to draw you near.

I'd sing about the traits I love ...
the things that make you shine,
and how I've wished for all these years
one day you would be mine.

I'd give my song a melody
like angels sing at times,
and fill it with the grandest words;
no elemental rhymes,

for any tune I'd sing to you
would need to make you smile,
and hopefully you'd want to stay
close by me for a while.

Perhaps I'd gather violins,
a harp, a cello too,
to illustrate the adoration
my heart feels for you.

Then I would fill the night with song ...
a song to melt your heart
and give you reasons to believe
we must not be apart.

And finally, I'd sing for you,
a song to make you weep
for all the years that could have been
sweet memories to keep.

The Unheard Song

I lift a pearly shell and hear
the ocean singing in my ear,
and dream of sailing to a distant isle
where you and I might someday be,
if not for an eternity,
together for at least a little while.

But if you cannot condescend
to change your life and gladly spend
a little time alone with only me,
I have no choice. I'll say goodbye
and never let you see me cry,
preserving, if I might, some dignity.

I toss the shell into the sea
along with dreams that cannot be,
and vow to pull my head out of the sand.
Why dream the dreams that won't come true
or dare to think you're someone who
would want to be with me? I understand.

Just like an ocean in a shell,
my soaring dreams have cast a spell
extending far beyond reality,
and, though I've loved you deep and long,
your heart has never heard the song
o'erwhelming me like music from the sea.

The Power of Silence

Bright words well up when beauty strikes the mind
and stirs the slumbered senses to ignite.
With words we speak of wonders we may find
and tell of things which give our souls delight.

It is with words we sing a song of joy
or seek to woo a lover to our side.
When trouble lurks, it's language we employ,
for words can heal ... or hinder and divide.

The power of a word is manifest
in many little ways throughout each day,
but how impactful are those moments blessed
with silence, filled with words we *didn't* say!

Within those quiet moments, some have learned
profundity is not by words discerned.

I Saw You

"Whoso loves, believes the impossible."
   - Elizabeth Barrett Browning

I saw you long before you realized I was there.
I watched you as you looked at her and smiled.
I couldn't help but notice how you touched her hair
and held her hand as gently as a child.

I think I fell in love just watching as you danced.
You softly sang the words against her ear.
How special she must feel, I thought, to be romanced
by one so handsome, charming and sincere.

She's never known the tears which loneliness can bring,
when love disdains a heart that knows not why.
Nor can she understand the bitter winds that sting,
as life becomes a desert, bleak and dry.

It was without surprise I felt the teardrops start
as, when the music ceased, you held her tight.
With eyes revealing all that overflowed your heart,
you promised her the world that starlit night.

I hadn't meant to listen, but I loved you too,
impossibly and hopelessly, it seemed,
and though I knew my fantasy could not come true,
you were the shining knight of which I'd dreamed.

I watched with silent envy as you left the floor
still holding her as if she were divine.
You looked around, then led her gently toward the door,
but for one endless beat, your eyes held mine.

You saw me, but you didn't see how much I cared,
nor could you have imagined my heart's pain,
as I accepted willingly, this love unshared
would be the only love my heart would gain.

A Candle in the Night

I light a candle in the night
and place it on the window sill,
unsure of what I hope to find,
but wishing to dispel the chill
of winter's stormy interlude.

My loneliness is like the night;
friends have deserted, children too,
and left me here inside these walls
with nothing much to see or do,
and where not even sounds intrude.

The candle flickers in the wind
and smoky wisps rise up like dreams
that used to burn with passion's flame
but now evaporate in steam,
as dark and daunting as my mood.

I watch the waning light and see
the candle pooling on the plate
and recognize with sinking heart
my time has gone. It is too late
for wishful dreams that might delude.

But there, within the wisps of smoke,
a face appears and seems to smile.
A shadowed vision hovers close
and lingers for a little while,
its smile with grace and peace imbued.

The candle now is almost gone,
but smoke still curls and floats about
the room, much like a tender friend
who's come to banish all the doubt
that would true happiness exclude.

I resolutely trim the wick
and find another match to light
the shrinking candle on the sill,
then realize, though it is night,
my waning hope has been renewed.

Since You Are Gone

Since you are gone, I've lost my way…
a lonely ship on starless seas,
no songs to sing, no words to say.
Since you are gone, I've lost my way.

What compass should this heart obey?
What tack to take to find a breeze?
Since you are gone, I've lost my way …
a lonely ship on starless seas.

Tears in the Dark

The place is dark. I'm certain you'll not notice I am there.
I've come once more to hear you play and ease my heart's despair.

The way you sing your mellow songs and strum your old guitar,
stirs something deep within my soul. I listen from afar,

secluded in my shadowed place as music fills the room,
and for a pleasant interlude, sweet love songs lift the gloom.

As you begin your set, the sounds surround me like a sea
of warmth and comfort I've not felt since you last sang to me.

Once, in my childish way, I thought you weren't worthy of
my heart's devotion and I spurned your tender gifts of love.

I let my foolish heart define the friendship we once shared
and only now, as I look back, I see how much you cared.

But that was long ago. Tonight I hope my heart can find
some self-forgiveness for that time when I was so unkind.

I listen as the music soars and patrons sing along
and suddenly I hear the notes of what was once our song.

The tears that fall unbidden from my eyes, I cannot hide,
and as the last notes fade away, you're standing by my side.

"I saw you in the shadows and a flood of memories
brought back that song," you whisper while you're dropping to your knees.

You pull me close and once again we share a warm embrace
as, with great tenderness, you brush the teardrops from my face.

"There is a time for letting go of all that wounds the heart,"
you say, and as my eyes meet yours, I feel the healing start.

Why?

Why is it, when I stand beside the lake,
the past surrounds like chilly mountain air?
Why do old memories, like bubbles, break
across the surface of my mind? I stare
into the water's depths and see you there.

Why must it be that I cannot forget
the time, so long ago, when we were young
and eager dreams were ours? Must I regret
the words unspoken, songs we left unsung?
Why could we not complete what we'd begun?

If healing comes with time's slow-drifting sands,
why does my heart feel broken once again,
as if I were a girl still holding hands
with innocence and love that would remain
beyond the grave? I struggle now in vain

to say goodbye to one I cannot leave.
Your heart still holds me, even though you're gone.
As winter nears, once more I've come to grieve
and search for strength ... the courage to go on.
I pray this night soon yields to gentler dawn.

Silent Dreams

I visited your grave again today
and brought along, once more, a small bouquet.

I took away the roses from the past
and watched the petals fall. Some dreams don't last.

But there, beside your stone, a budding tree
gave shade and beauty and some hope to me.

The dreams we held fell silent in the grave,
but comforting me still ... the love you gave.

In Tender Light

When night is ending and the morning waits
to break my sleepy silence, through the hush,
I feel your presence near; your love creates
a glow preceding sunrise. With her brush,

sweet nature paints pastels across the sky,
then sets the clouds aflame with crimson light,
while in the shadows, by the window, I
can see you standing, brown eyes shining bright.

I know, when I reach out to touch your hand,
you'll come and place your eager lips on mine.
No words are spoken, yet we understand,
the warmth between us, sun cannot outshine.

So many are the mornings, come and gone,
since first you pledged your love long years ago,
yet here, beneath the tender light of dawn,
your kiss still sets my waking heart aglow.

My Gift for You

If I could capture morning's dawn
and put it in a present just for you,
I'd pack horizon's gold and red
along with sheen of light on roses' dew.

I'd not forget the wisp of moon
who seeks to sneak away so stealthily,
as if, in faded gown, she dare
not mingle with such regal company,

and if I could, I'd try to keep
the streaks of clouds that catch the suns first rays,
the way I sense your love each morn
before its warmth arrives to bless my days.

But I must hurry to seal up
this gift I know you'll want to hold awhile,
for dawn is but a fleeting kiss …
and then the sun appears with radiant smile.

Across the Sea

She plucks a fragrant rose from off the vine
and tucks it in her bonnet's lacy band,
then walks with graceful step, the dampened strand
along the great Pacific's azure brine.
The sun sinks low in evening's swift decline.
She sees her lonely footprints in the sand,
remembering the time, when hand in hand,
they strolled beneath the last rays' golden shine.

The one for whom she'd give most anything,
her much-missed sailor, ponders plaintively ...
"I wonder if she wears my friendship ring,
and though I love her, will she wait for me?"
He does not know each evening she will fling
a rose, her promise floating on the sea.

Waves of Memory

I hear the broken notes of distant song
adrift upon the wrinkled reach of sea
and listen as our voices sing along
once more in treasured realms of memory.

It's been too long since we, as carefree friends,
ran barefoot on the beach where seagulls play
and wrote our love in sand, with sticks as pens …
sweet promises we meant to keep some day.

But just as waves erased our heartfelt scrawls,
in time, you drifted to another shore.
Yet in my heart, your tender love still calls
and brings me to the singing sea once more.

The breeze conveys your touch across the years,
while in the sea spray, I still taste our tears.

I Saw a Heart

I saw a heart-shaped lake someplace --
it seemed as big as oceans are.
The sky was mirrored on its face
and in its depths there shone a star.

The moon skipped by and kissed each wave.
I laughed to see them blush and swell
and wondered how you might behave
if I should kiss your cheek as well.

For I have looked into your heart
and found it filled with love and grace,
as beautiful as any star
that decorates the realms of space ...

and I have gazed into your eyes
and glimpsed a mind as vast and deep
as any ocean, I'd surmise,
and warm with friendship I could keep.

A heart-shaped lake is rare to find,
but not so rare, it seems to me,
as finding one whose heart and mind
are wide and bright as any sea.

Evening Music at the Lake

The quaking aspens shake their silver leaves
like paper bells as evening breezes
dance across the lake's gray surface,
stirring gentle swells that splash the pebbled shore.
The coo-hoo-hoo of owls is like a love song
softly sung among the shadows of the branches high above.

The descant of the sighing breeze, the rustle of the trees,
the owls' low harmonies accompanied
by timpani of rocking water on the bow of anchored boats ~
are all melodic notes that play
the unique music of the evening.

A Fractal Heart

A fractal heart is not a broken heart ...
it is a heart whose love is infinite.

No matter how much it loves,
there is always more love to give.

Its love is beyond mathematical formulas
or science's ability to measure.
It is love without limits.

Its depths cannot be plumbed;
its character endures
and duplicates itself,
multiplying countless times
in those who know its love.

Some have said its shape
is the shape of God's thumbprint.

Its extraordinary beauty
stuns the mind.

Search for its end
and you will not find it.
Seek its beginning,
and you may actually find
the fathomless heart of God.

Heart Gifts

I was surprised to find today
upon my porch, with ribbon tied,
an elegant rosebud bouquet.
I carried it inside.

With buds arranged in vase of bronze,
I peered outside through frosted pane.
Snow covered all the neighbors' lawns ...
no movement marred the plane.

I wondered who had left these gifts
without a card explaining why,
nor were there footprints in the drifts,
no car seen passing by ...

Yet such a lovely thing to find
wrapped up and waiting by my door.
Who left them there? I searched my mind ...
a friend I'd known before?

Just then the phone began to ring.
I ran to answer in the hall,
but though I waited, listening,
I heard no sound at all.

At last there was a quiet sniff,
a muffled sob and then a sigh.
I couldn't help but feel as if
I too might start to cry.

Instead I spoke into the phone,
a simple thank you for the gift.
Although, once more, I was alone,
I felt my sorrow lift.

I understood who, in the night,
had come before the midnight snow
and left me roses, red and white,
tied with a satin bow.

He did not want my thanks, I'd guess.
His call was simply to make sure
I'd found the roses on my steps.
His motives were quite pure.

He understood the pain I felt.
His life's companion too, had died.
The loneliness with which we dwelt
can take a toll inside.

Although I hadn't ventured out
since my own loved one passed away,
at last I saw, life is about
the gifts we share each day.

I dug into my freezer's store
and found a turkey roast to bake,
then called my grieving friend before
I made a chocolate cake.

He came, reluctantly I thought,
for his loyal heart was still in pain,
but for a while, we both forgot
our grief and smiled again.

haiku (wind song sweeps)

wind song sweeps
through crowd of pines on hillside
nature's flash mob

haiku (rainbow trout)

giant rainbow trout
breaks water's mirrored surface
fisherman's good luck

haiku (tree branches draw)

tree branches draw
black lace across pink sunset
dream catcher's web

Tanka (afternoon shadows)

afternoon shadows
move together on the lawn
as night approaches
my love reaches out for you
beyond the pale horizon

Songs of Gratitude

Awakened by the finches' cheerful songs,
I swing my feet out, touch the chilly floor,
and crouch before the open window sash.
The rosy blush of morning lights the sky

and warms the edges of the steel-gray clouds.
I feel the cooling breeze against my face
and shiver in the beauty of the moment.
How good of God to wake us with His touch!

I'm moved by all the sights and sounds which greet
my eyes and ears this glowing summer morn.
My heart is overflowing with such joy,
compelling me to join the finches' choir.

How else might I express my gratitude
or share the praise that overflows my soul?
So, unconstrained, I lift my song to Him
who fills each day and night with wondrous gifts.

The playful breeze envelops every note
and carries each, as if on angel wings,
to mingle with the birds' bright melodies
and finally, to brush the ear of God.

The Path We Travel

Sometimes the path we travel
beneath the sunlit skies,
leads through the trees whose canopies
shield golden butterflies.

Sometimes the path is narrow,
where only one can go ...
through valleys cold where flowers fold
as evening sun sinks low.

Sometimes the path is steep
and difficult to climb.
No footprints show the way to go
and shadows alter time.

Sometimes we are not able
to carry on alone.
Our last strength fails and dark prevails.
No path at all is shown.

But there is One to guide us
when we are lost or cold.
He knows the way through night *or* day
and lends His hand to hold.

Forest Musings

One day I walked along a forest trail
and saw a doe and fawn in shadow near.
I stopped to rest beneath a shady pine
and wait awhile, lest I disturb the deer.

I watched the spotted babe drink thirstily
from mother's teats and marveled at God's plan ...
how He provides for every creature's needs,
that none should be in want, not beast nor man.

I thought of how the chipmunk's tiny claws
can find the hidden nuts within a cone;
how birds find worms beneath the moistened soil
and bees know how to build a honeycomb.

I saw how every plant in season blooms,
then shares its fruit and multiplies its seed
and how the heavens give both light and rain
to satisfy each organism's need.

If ever I should wonder about God,
the evidence is clear, my soul declares.
He loves his children with a perfect love,
fills all our needs and then makes us his heirs.

I soon resumed my walk along the trail
and smiled to feel the warmth of morning sun,
reminding me that all things here below
are blessed by God whose love warms everyone.

Creation

~ Isaiah 40

God cupped His hand and measured out
the waters of the sea.
His outstretched palm determined just
how wide the sky should be.

He filled a basket full of dust
and mixed in loam and sand,
then poured it forth across the earth,
creating the dry land.

He weighed some portions out with care
to make the rolling hills
and heaped majestic mountains high
with His creative skills.

All nature sings at His command.
The wind and waves obey.
The stars shine forth to pierce the dark
and sun illumines day.

What mortal dares to counsel Him,
to teach him what is right?
His thoughts are higher than our thoughts,
His ways-- my soul's delight.

A Quiet Path

I strolled a quiet path one day
along the shores of Monterey
and there I found, to my immense surprise,
an artist sitting all alone
upon a cold and craggy stone,
in silence, contemplating azure skies.

I asked him why no color showed
upon his canvas. Dark eyes glowed
as he replied he could not find a way
to duplicate the sights he saw.
God's art filled him with so much awe.
I bowed my head, not knowing what to say,

for I had felt these things as well,
while sensing I'd a tale to tell,
yet knowing I could not, with my weak pen,
describe the wondrous depths of love
which flows each day from God above.
In awe, I search for words, but can't begin.

I left him there, his brush in hand,
and found a seat on crumpled sand
to watch the shining ocean ebb and flow,
and as I watched, it seemed to me
my Lord was walking on the sea.
The words He spoke soon set my heart aglow.

"Man cannot equal God, it's true,
but I have given gifts to you
which you may use to glorify my name.
Surrender mind and heart to me
and when you lift your pen, you'll see
my words will kindle inspiration's flame."

I watched the sinking sun dip low,
and wondered if this could be so.
Was this God's way of causing doubts to cease?
Just then the ocean waves grew calm,
their whisper on the sand, a psalm
of gratitude that filled my heart with peace.

Perhaps God walked upon the sea
and spoke in patient love to me,
that I, at last, might come to understand ...
I'm human; my best works are flawed
and can't compare to those of God,
but somehow they are blessed by His great hand.

Finding Beauty

If you should ask me where true beauty lies,
I'd look about for something God has done ...
the crimson hues adorning evening skies,
or lilies lit by rays of morning sun.

But others, I am sure, would disagree.
They'd tell you beauty rests in human form ...
a young girl's face with perfect symmetry
or eyes so kind they make a cold heart warm.

Perhaps the truth lies somewhere in between.
Where God is found, there beauty sheds her grace,
and we, with hearts as well as eyes, have seen
His touch upon the world, or on a face.

Wherever beauty lies, we can agree,
to savor it is our priority.

The Birth

To hold a baby born to me,
to count the toes
and feel the tiny fingers close
around my own,
creates a sea of ecstasy
henceforth unknown.

To hold a poem born to me,
to count the feet
and feel the pulsing rhythm beat
within my brain,
is ecstasy ... a mystery
I can't explain.

Writing is a Lark

I've known a happiness that numbs the mind
to all the cares this hectic world might bring.
I've found a joy few souls may ever find ...
a joy that makes both larks and poets sing.

Our feathered friends are stirred to rhapsody
by simple things. The crimson clouds at dawn,
a rainbow's light, a mate's bright melody,
or insects found beneath the dewy lawn.

But poets too, must sing and so it goes ...
A rosy sky, a songbird in the night,
a heart so filled with love it overflows,
all move the willing poet's pen to write,

and as he writes, the magic in each word
becomes a lark, a song that must be heard.

Disclaimer

Don't read my words and try to fit
them neatly to my life.

I am the sort whose heart beats with
the world's. Her joy, her strife

are mine. I see a hungry child
and weep as though its mother --

or learn a soldier died at war,
and mourn as if a brother.

Emily Dickinson

She moved so softly through the world,
the air was barely stirred ...
yet everything within her sight
was carefully observed
and captured in a word.

The unknown aggregate of heaven,
the mystery of death,
a bee's elusive qualities,
and love's unfathomed depth,
all gave her poems breath.

The eloquence that issued from
her heart and mind, her hand
recorded faithfully, for friends
who didn't understand,
but sensed that it was grand.

And finally, when she believed
her work was nearly o'er,
she stitched her poems into books
and locked them in a drawer,
then paused to write some more.

Love Is a Poem

Love is a poem that sings to me
Magically setting my spirit free.
Nothing can quiet the melody
Or quench stolen moments of poetry...
Moments that stretch to infinity.

Nothing can measure the joy love brings
Or silence the songs a full heart sings.
Poetry soars on ethereal wings,
Quietly turning the humblest of things
Into a treasure sufficient for kings.

Unexpected Gifts

Your calming words,
like whispered waves from ocean's deep,
caress my mind
and leave behind a wisdom I can keep.

Your loving heart,
like treasured volumes on my shelf,
engenders joy ...
each opened page a gift I give myself.

No Words

A poet pulls his words from lofty air
and writes a rhyme both eloquent and sweet.
A parrot gathers words from others' lips
and what he hears, he soon learns to repeat.

But when I long to tell you of my love
and how it overflows my heart each day,
I find I know not where to turn for words ...
I want to speak, but cannot find a way.

An orator, in language rich and deep,
expounds with care, selecting every word,
and even children make their wishes known
in words they're sure are understood and heard.

But when I am with you, my heart, so full,
can find no way to tell you how I feel.
There are no words it seems, that can explain
this love so indescribable, yet real.

Instead, I simply sit in silent awe
and marvel that you love me as you do.
I fear you'll never know the gratitude
and overwhelming love I feel for you.

A Path So Rare

One day I stumbled on a path
that led, I knew not where,
but when I bravely followed it,
I found a poet there.

He jumped out from the junipers
and gave me such a start,
I laughed at first, but cried some too.
His poems touched my heart.

He wrote of scaling mountain heights
and love along the way,
of flowers bright, like stars at night
and dreams to light the day.

He taught me of a magic world
where love flows like a river,
where knighthood lives with chivalry
and everyone's a giver.

I loved the life he showed me there
inside his magic land
and happily I followed when
he took me by the hand

and led me deeper down the path
beyond the shrubs and flowers,
to sit beside a waterfall
where time, unmarked by hours,

slipped silently beyond our sight
as if there were no time,
but only love and poetry,
and friendship so sublime.

I cannot tell you where I've been
nor where that path was found,
but I am sure the place is real,
although I was spellbound.

You Are the One

When days are bright and filled with laughter,
you are the one who makes me smile.
Yours is the heart I can depend on …
beautiful heart that knows no guile.

When doubts assail and I'm uncertain,
striving to squelch my unnamed fears,
you are the one whose strength I count on …
you are the one who sees my tears.

You are the one who lends me wisdom,
sharing your light when paths grow dim.
You are the one who, in the darkness,
bids me to pause and sing a hymn.

You are the one who never fails me.
You are the one who takes my hand
and guides me gently through the sorrows
that only you can understand.

You are the one who truly knows me.
You are the one who's always there.
I can't imagine life without you!
Yours is the love I'm blessed to share.

Unseen Love

There is a quiet love that dwells unseen ...
unnoticed deep beneath the drifting snow.
It waits in silent hope for coming spring
and heaven's sun to set its face aglow.

Like flowers lying dormant, without glory,
such love is ready, when the snows have ceased,
to open and to tell its own sweet story ...
its fragrance and soft beauty soon released.

Just such a love I found one early dawn
as dark clouds parted and the waiting sun
spread unexpected warmth; my tears were gone
and love filled every nook where once was none!

I write this little song to let you know
the love you wakened in my frozen heart,
much like the flowers waiting under snow,
reveals its fragrant gifts as each day starts.

I Thought of You

I saw three sparrows in a blossomed tree.
Their cheerful song was beautiful to hear.
I thought of you and love's soft melody
alive within my heart each time you're near.

Two sparrows flew away into the sky.
The one they left behind soon ceased his song.
I thought of how you fill my life, but I
can hear no music anytime you're gone.

The blossoms on the tree were white with pink ...
a snowy cloud against the sky of blue.
I thought of how you color all I think ...
how beautiful my world because of you!

And then I thought of life without a spring,
when winter winds snatch blossoms from the tree
and sparrows tuck their heads beneath their wings.
How bare and cold without you life would be!

Silence Reigns

Your voice once filled my days with light.
Now silence reigns.
Your absence echoes through the night
as tears remain
un-dried, and sorrow, once unknown,
now seeps like pain, through every bone.
No arms enfold. I weep in vain,
as silence reigns.

Your words had power to ignite
my passion's flame;
my soaring spirit found new heights
as love became
our food and drink, our everything,
the melodies love's songbirds sing
each time I'd hear you speak my name.
Now silence reigns.

The Mockingbird's Song

Why does the mockingbird sing in the night
while the world is so dark and still?
Why does his song sound so blissfully bright,
though the moon slipped over the hill?

Why does the mockingbird high in the tree,
where branches dance softly in time,
give voice in the darkness to pure melody,
a music so sweetly sublime?

Perhaps there's a reason his gentle heart sings,
though others are nowhere in sight.
His song carries hope on invisible wings
and promises all will be right.

For those who are lonely and some who are sad
or wondering why life goes on,
the mockingbird's song must surely make glad
those hearts ever longing for dawn.

Eventually

Eventually the day will come again
when sun will warm and dogwood trees will bloom.
Eventually we'll have enough of rain
and dreary nights where hearts get lost in gloom.

Eventually the clouds will drift away
and stars will once again be free to shine.
The moon, though shadowed, will be on display,
sweet symbol of a fragile love, once mine.

I linger by the window, pen in hand
and wait for something beautiful to sing,
but birds are still, as if they understand
there are no longer songs worth mentioning.

I scribble words with neither rhyme nor sense,
but find a growing peace envelops me.
Though darkness gathers, there is mute defense
in writing random words of poetry.

Eventually the lark will spread her wings
and soar as if she'd never need to land,
and I, as well, will rise to soar and sing.
Rare is the pain the spirit can't withstand.

Flecks of Gold

A miner kneels beside the rushing stream
and dips his pan into the shallow flow.
When tilted toward the sun, a sudden gleam
reveals the tiny golden flakes aglow.

He's found precisely what he's looking for,
and so, with pounding heart, he dips again
and adds more treasure to his growing store,
until the light is gone and night creeps in.

It is the same with friendships, I have found.
The golden flakes of joy pile one on one
where streams of kindness flow and love abounds,
until at last, we yield to setting sun.

But who can say such treasures found below
may not, in Heaven's realm, more brightly glow?

Little Things

A friend is one who sings your song
when there's no music in the air,
who stays with you the whole night long,
when you're too weak to know she's there.

A friend is one who hears your cry
when you're too proud to show your tears
and offers comfort, shares a sigh,
and helps you push beyond your fears.

A friend is one who pleads your case
when all the world has turned away,
and never waivers in her faith
that you'll be proven right someday.

A friend gives love both pure and free,
not seeking earthly recompense.
Some call them "little things." To me
these are true gifts, beyond immense.

Friendship River

A river swept me off my feet
and carried me away,
past pretty houses painted neat
where little children play …
past swaying trees with trembling leaves
where birds sang endlessly
and graveyards where the lonely grieve
with tears for what can't be.

My river grew to be a friend
which buoyed me with its song,
from mountain lakes to valleys end
and where the sea belonged.
From where I rode, I viewed the skies
and all that lined the shore,
and saw afresh with heart's keen eyes
what I'd not seen before.

For drifting through the world alone,
without a friend to care,
I'd missed the love I might have known
and all the beauty there.
But riding high upon the crest
of River's willing tide,
I saw love's purpose at its best
and felt its joy inside.

The love of friends is measureless,
and like the endless river,
brings gifts that will, with pleasure, bless
recipient and giver.
My river circles endlessly,
its waters deep and swift.
Because of you, I'm blessed to be
receiver of its gift.

The Widow and the Wren

A small, brown wren lands on my window sill
and stares with his unblinking, beady eyes.
I offer bread crumbs, wondering if he will
be frightened by my overwhelming size.

I only wish him well. Then, as he flies
I want to ask if he'll return one day,
or roam forever through the cloudless skies,
but he is off, not caring what I say.

A stranger in a parking lot one night
asks sadly if I have a buck to spare.
I wonder why it is he thinks I might,
and if I say I've nothing, will he care?

But life is strange. I'd feed a flighty wren
and not give something to a hungry man?
The wren has flown and won't return again.
I pause a moment, then devise a plan.

I ask the one who only begged a dollar,
if he would like to join me for a meal.
He seems unnerved and, tugging at his collar,
reminds me he's unwashed. How would I feel

to dine with one who's ragged and unclean?
I reassure him it is no big deal.
It doesn't matter much with whom I'm seen.
What matters more is that he needs a meal.

And so it was, I had a friend that night.
He shared his story and my heart was blessed
to spend some time with one who soon took flight …
a wounded wren who'd fallen from his nest.

The Coming of Snow

The morning waits just past the edge of night.
Awakening, I listen to the hush
and sense the air is filled with silent snow.
No breath of breeze disturbs its feathered fall.

Anticipation fills my waiting mind ...
anticipation for the pristine view,
when dawn first filters through the evergreens
and lights the world beyond my window pane,

but also for the first glimpse of your smile,
the smile which lights your eyes and stirs my heart.
So like the quiet snow, you fill my world
with all that's bright and pure and nobly good.

You gently cover all my flaws with love.
It floats into my life with quiet calm
and graciously makes beautiful somehow,
what heretofore was desolate and bare.

The morning light reveals a fairyland
of sparkling crystal as the flakes subside.
Each drooping limb and blade is velvet soft,
the scene transformed, aglow with rosy dawn.

And so it is, your touch transforms my life.
My heart is ever grateful for the way
you came, with layers of deep love, and made
what once was marred, seem elegant and pure.

You Alone

You came when I silently called
and heard what my lips couldn't speak.
You held my hand in the darkness
and swept away tears from my cheek.

You alone understood why I trembled,
why the midnight frightened me so,
and you whispered your comforting words,
telling secrets I did not know.

Though you ached with the pain of my sorrow,
you assured me a new day would shine
and all that seemed hopeless and bitter
would vanish. Soon joy would be mine.

You promised you'd always stay near me
though everyone else turned away.
You're the one who sought help from the Father
when I was too weary to pray.

It was you who brought elegant music
into the stillness of fear
and taught me to dance in the moonlight,
holding me lovingly near.

So, now that the storm clouds have parted
and sunlight is bathing the earth,
you're the friend to whom I'm devoted...
a friend of unparalleled worth.

I Saw a Friendship

I saw a friendship like a rose
whose bud was still encased in green,
wrapped tightly as a tiny gift,
its magnitude as yet unseen.

I watered it all through the night
awaiting sunlight's warming rays,
and soon the bloom with beauty shone,
and fragrance wafted through my days.

I saw a friendship like a tree.
It grew inside a grove and shared
its shade in leafy canopies
where secrets safely could be bared

and where, when life was crowding in,
a soul could seek some solitude
and listen to sweet poetry,
secure from all that would intrude.

I saw a friendship like a cloud
that seemed to float beyond my touch,
yet gave to earth its cleansing rain
or winter snow that hid so much

of what would have been visible,
were it not kindly shielded so;
for who has not seen weeds transformed
to beauty by the touch of snow?

I saw a friendship, beautiful
as any rose or towering tree,
as giving as a winter cloud,
for all the love it offered me.

The Word Goodbye

"Parting is all we know of heaven
and all we need of hell."
~~Emily Dickinson

There is a sadness in the word goodbye ...
a loneliness that follows, and a sigh
to break the heart of those whose love is deep.
It is no wonder farewells make us weep.

There is a pain that sears a breaking heart
when those who love find they must be apart.
To say goodbye and know you may not see
your loved one 'til you breach eternity,

is more of anguish than a heart should know.
And so, with tears, I beg you not to go,
for suddenly it seems I cannot bear
to wake at night and know you are not there.

So many years you've been a part of me,
and by your leaving, you remove the key
that opens up my heart to love's soft shine ...
the glow your presence brings, no longer mine.

The melodies we shared have disappeared
and smiles are washed away by threatening tears.
My heart cannot accept the word goodbye.
Please hold me one more time before I cry.

Where Do You Put a Broken Heart?

I place the dishes on the shelf,
fill up the washer, pull to start,
collect the books, and ask myself,
"Where shall I put this broken heart?"

I glue the rocker's arm with care,
replace the blender's missing part,
then mend the blouse I plan to wear,
but who will mend this tattered heart?

I run my errands, plan the meals
and heap the groceries in my cart.
I wonder if the checker feels
the pain that fills my aching heart.

Hearts break, and somehow life goes on.
The birds still sing, the stars still shine.
The earth revolves from dark to dawn,
but what will heal this heart of mine?

Little Moments

The night is long because you are not in it.
You are my sun, my warmth, my brilliant light.
You're in my heart, my thoughts, each waking minute.
You fill my dreams when I'm asleep at night.

The moon peeks in my open window blind
and seems to smile. The stars, too, wink their eyes
as if to say, "We know what's on your mind,
and soon he will return, like dawn's bright skies."

But when the nights are dark, that's when I dream
the dream that says this loneliness will end ...
that we, together, may become a team
and I become much more to you than friend.

Until that day, I'll try to be content
with little moments in your presence spent.

Folded Dreams

The chaplain's gone; the bugler too.
The stained glass window of a cross
casts hallowed light across the pew
where one still struggles with her loss.

To honor all their dreams, now broken,
and the folded flag, small token
of gratitude for all he gave,
she dries her tears. She will be brave.

The Farmer's Son

The rows of corn stretched wide across the field.
The farmer's son moved silently among
the ripened ears and plucked the golden yield
of labors he and father had begun.

The road stretched long. Ahead, a desert storm.
The farmer's son marched proudly, head held high.
A soldier now, in dust-caked uniform,
he'd bravely serve his country, even die.

The rows of crosses stretched across the lawn
and up the hill that overlooked the sea.
The farmer's son lay silent, battle won ...
a small, white cross to mark his victory.

The farmer labors still, amidst the corn,
but never does a single day pass by
when he does not remember, pause and mourn
the son he loved, who bravely went ... to die.

Welcome Home

Today a soldier rode in a parade.
The crowd cried "Welcome home!" with loud applause,
to thank him for the courage he'd displayed
in bravely fighting for a noble cause.

Across the town another soldier rode
in silence. No applause or raucous cheers
would welcome him to this, his new abode ...
this flag-draped coffin stained with sorrow's tears.

While one man waved his country's flag and smiled,
the other could not see the flag he bore,
but through their tears, his grieving wife and child
saw something they'd not understood before ...

His "Welcome home!" was in another place ...
at home at last, with Jesus, face to face.

A Golden Gift

One day, in confidence, I shared
a sorrow overwhelming me.
I felt the loneliness of grief,
a broken heart's immensity.

Soon after, came an envelope.
Not knowing what my eyes might see,
I found an unexpected gift
wrapped up in words meant just for me.

I read the words so sweetly penned
and felt the love behind each letter
spelled out with care and kind concern …
some words to help my heart feel better.

I read the lines with tear-filled eyes …
"When your heart breaks, mine's broken too,"
and though he said, "It's only words,"
the words and music both came through

and touched me with their magnitude
and graceful generosity.
How could I be so blessed to find
a friend who'd sing such songs to me?

My heart, though wounded by life's pain,
now overflows with love's warm touch,
as someone many miles away
reached out to me and gave so much;

a golden gift wrapped up in words,
and underneath the words, a song
that sang its way into my heart
and gave me comfort, made me strong.

Cradled in the Paleness of the Moon

Cradled in the paleness of the moon,
snuggled in the stillness of the night,
lulled by poems in the wind, I soon
close my eyes to wait for morning light.

Winking quietly from high above,
stars remember where the dreams are kept,
sending them to dreamers lost in love.
Waking now, I wonder if I've slept.

Near me lies the one who knows my heart,
holding all my life in love's embrace.
Understanding bound us from the start ...
carried us together to this place

somewhere near the edge of earthly time,
while the world slips silently away.
Now we're nearer to that home sublime,
where dawn will welcome never-ending day.

Might we go together, he and I?
Life, for me, is death without his charms.
If, perchance, I am the first to die,
may sweet mem'ries fill his empty arms.

Cradled in the paleness of the moon,
snuggled in the stillness of the night,
lulled by poems in the wind, I'll soon
close my eyes to wait for dawn's pure light.

The End of Day

We sit together, faces toward the west,
where nature paints the day's demise with rose,
and one by one, emboldened stars divest
themselves of daylight's worn and faded clothes

and lend their beauty to the darkening night.
I feel your hand take mine and instantly
the old familiar awe, the sheer delight
of your sweet presence washes over me.

The night is soon alive with wind chimes' tune
as breezes move the summer air aside
with cooling strokes. A wisp of smiling moon
peeks through the trees, its beauty un-denied.

"How fresh and pure the evening seems," you say.
I feel so blessed to have you in my world
and know somehow, beyond the close of day,
when sun sinks low and winking stars unfurl,

I'll feel you ever close in mind and heart.
Your smile will never fade from memory.
Not life, nor death can tear our souls apart,
or ever steal the love you've given me.

Knitted Together

When two have cared as we have cared,
and deep love shared,
we cannot be
just you and me.

For, through the years we have become,
not two, but one.
Our knitted hearts
won't come apart.

When two hearts know, as we have known,
how close we've grown,
the bond is sure
and will endure.

Her Comforter

With tear-filled eyes she searched horizon's haze
beyond the water's churning blues and grays,
but not a sign of life could she perceive
to comfort her.

With broken heart she knew the aching truth ...
the one she'd loved since tender days of youth
could no more hold her close, or hurts relieve,
to comfort her.

The ageless waters bathed the stony shore
the way her tears would flow forevermore.
There were not years enough in which to grieve,
or comfort her.

The one who'd been her rock, her guiding light,
had sailed on silent wings into the night.
Yet there remained one hope to which she'd cleave
to comfort her.

The words she'd heard all through her growing years,
like washing waves, repeated in her ears:
"God loves you more than mind has yet conceived."
He'd comfort her.

To this she clung, and found at last, sweet peace.
Assured this pain would end and joy increase,
she knew God cared, for He too was bereaved;
her Comforter.

God's Embrace

When sorrows come and skies turn strangely dim,
when nothing in my life is going right,
when I have lost my way, I turn to Him.
He knows the path and gladly shares His light.

So many times He's lifted my despair
and sent His sunlight through the cloudy skies.
Disrupting chilling storms, He clears the air
and hangs a rainbow there before my eyes.

How could He love a wayward child this much ...
to paint once rainy skies with every hue
and with His tender love, reach down to touch
a weary soul who knows not what to do?

When sorrows come, I seek His shining face
and wait to feel once more His kind embrace.

My Girl

In the early morning hush,
my boots clank against the boards
as I stride to the edge of the veranda
and gaze out across the misty acres of the ranch.

There is a surprising beauty in the high desert,
beauty as far as a man can see.
My eyes take in the landscape,
the low hills white with last night's snowfall,
the jutting rocks, their edges softened now,
and the scrubby cedars with their gauzy dusting of white.

I can hear the tumbling waters of the narrow river
just down the slope, and far off in the distance,
the muffled moos of the herd.

A dove calls softly from the tall pine beside the house,
but as usual, it is the sky that captures my attention.
I'm amazed by its ever-changing mood,
a complete circle of light, uninterrupted by humans,
much like a man's thoughts on a lonely ride.

This morning I'm just in time to see the first rays of sun
break beneath the clouds on the eastern horizon,
painting the snowy scene with shades of pink and yellow.

I lift my steaming mug of coffee between my palms
and breathe in its strong aroma while it warms my hands.
The smell of it, along with the biting cold of the morning,
makes me think of roundup time,
Anna there beside me, brewing coffee over a campfire
and frying bacon and eggs for the cowhands.
The memory is fragrant and warm, like my coffee.

I see Treble, my mare, down by the river,
pawing snow from a tuft of grass.
How patiently she's waited, un-ridden
while I cared for my precious Anna.

Ah, my darling girl, my wife, how I miss her!
How I wish she were here with me still ...

But I know it isn't kind to wish her back.
Her suffering is finally over
and I like to imagine she's sitting quietly at Jesus' feet
asking Him all the questions that filled her brilliant mind.

I set my mug on the railing
and with the backs of my hands,
brush the tears from my cheeks.
After a long moment,
I place two fingers between my lips
and give a shrill whistle.
The mare lifts her head and looks my way,
then takes a few hesitant steps toward the house.

"Come on, girl," I call and she quickens her pace,
leaving marks in the fresh snow as she climbs the slope.

I lift the bridle from its hook
and slip it smoothly over the mare's head,
sensing her anticipation ... and mine.

With a familiar pleasure, I hoist
saddle and blanket onto her back
and cinch the strap around her barrel.
She shivers with excitement,
her breath turning to mist in the crispy air.

We trot easily along the packed trail beside the river,
the sound of her hoof beats in rhythm
with the song of the rushing waters.

"It's just you and me now, old girl,"
I say to the mare, my voice husky.
She lifts her ears and turns her head to look at me.
I lean forward and give her neck a pat,
putting slack in the reins.
My knees tighten against her ribs.

I sense she knows my heart, much as my Anna did.
With a joyous lunge, she breaks into a full gallop.
This will do us both good.

The powdery snow flies up behind us
and the icy wind rushes into my face,
bringing fresh tears to my old eyes.

Although We Grieve

I took a tempting path into a wood
where sunlight filtered through the colored leaves,
and there, in dappled shade, I understood
why life somehow goes on, although we grieve.

Soft memories of you still fill my heart.
I see you in the shadows and the sun
and wonder why we have to be apart.
For me, there'll never be another one.

But even though my arms won't ever know
again the loving warmth of your embrace,
the sun still shines and broken hearts don't show.
I've learned to hide the teardrops on my face.

Although we grieve, life somehow stumbles on,
and darkest night is followed by the dawn.

At Morning Light

There is a certain majesty
at morning light,
a scene akin to fantasy
when all seems right.
The promise of the coming day
holds evening's dark concerns at bay
and frees the bird of hope for flight,
at morning light.

As shadows shorten and we see
with fresh insight,
how promising the day may be,
a calm delight
infuses every heart with peace
and makes the simplest joys increase,
at morning light.

God's Presence

He speaks to me in joy.
I hear His voice in the winter winds
that whip through the valley
and bend the meadow grasses low.

He wraps me in His peace.
I see His hand on the mountain side
where the rocks and trees
stand hushed in the soft, new-fallen snow.

He comes to me with love.
I feel His heart in the drumming rain
on a summer day,
and find His light in the rainbow's glow.

He calls me to Himself.
His voice resounds through the pounding surf
at the ocean's edge,
and my soul responds; I am His, I know!

Lonely Sonnet

Horizon's distant line, I've never crossed,
where ocean spills into some great abyss.
When I approach, the line is blurred or lost.
Although I think I'm close, somehow I miss.

How similar it seems, when love is near.
I sail the sea with open heart and mind,
my destination visible and clear,
so ready to embrace the love I find.

But just about the time when I begin
to feel I have true love within my reach,
I find myself alone, adrift again
somewhere between the heavens and the beach.

It seems that love, much like horizon's line,
is but a dream beyond this heart of mine.

White Sails

I
As white sails move and billow in the breeze,
the boat, in silence, skims the frothy waves.
I watch with wonder from my shoreline copse
and listen to the wind among the branches.

It sings to me of robust, youthful joy,
and sun-filled days once billowing with love.
Our hearts, so full, seemed borne on golden wings
which carried us above life's tribulations.

But somehow joy was lost, for with a cry,
the love we shared was shattered like a swan
pierced through its heart with sorrow's tainted bullet.
You left before the winter snowflakes fell.

Although you never knew how much it hurt,
kind memories bring peace and love still soars.

II
Kind memories bring peace and love still soars,
as even now, I hold you in my heart,
and when I am alone in secret thought,
I reminisce as if you never left.

The pain of loss dissolves away with time
and lifeless sails that once, so listless, hung
unmoving in the stillness of the night,
have found again the stirring winds of joy.

I may not soar, unbridled as a youth,
for age and reason bring a tempered tone,
but I am nudged by hope and quiet love ...
enough to keep this aging craft on course.

Remembering our love, my heart is filled,
as white sails move and billow in the breeze.

I Would Not Dare

I would not dare to ask a dream of you,
someone so far beyond my narrow reach.
My mind could not believe you'd care for me
enough to share my walk on life's wide beach

where waves of loneliness crashed on the cliffs
and threatened to o'erwhelm my trembling soul.
But you appeared from where horizon gleamed
and offered an escape from slippery shoal.

I would not dare to dream you might remain
until the storms had passed and seas were calm.
Yet here you are, and hope rides on the tide
as I lift up my voice in grateful psalm.

For in your heart, I've found both love and light
and in your arms contentment never known.
I dare not ask, but you forestall the need,
with kind assurance I'll not sail alone.

Goodbye, Orvieto

I stand in the shade of the ancient duomo
and gaze down the hill where I see
a small, quiet figure alone in the sun.
He seems to be smiling at me.

I've come here because, of the places I've been,
there's one I could never forget --
Orvieto, the town that gave birth to a love
that lives in my heart even yet.

The memories are vivid, as if yesterday,
I stood in this very same place.
Before the sun set and the shadows grew deep,
he gently brushed tears from my face

and promised me we would eventually be
together forever. So much
I wanted to say, but I knew as he left,
I'd never forget his kind touch.

The man in the street at the foot of the hill
begins his ascent up the way,
and as he draws nearer, my heart leaps for joy.
For a moment, I'm back in that day,

reliving the memorable pleasures we'd shared,
the promises made and the dreams
to somehow return to this magical place.
Today is the day, but it seems

that life has played tricks and I cannot believe
the vision approaching me now;
a strange duplication of one I once loved,
but amazingly younger somehow.

Though I have grown older, the years have been kind.
I've lived with so few real regrets.
I've cherished our friendship. The letters he wrote
were light, charming stories; vignettes

of a life lived in joy in his country of birth,
the place he called "Bella Italia."
And I, with my memories of falling in love,
remember with fondest nostalgia

the evenings we spent underneath crystal skies,
our laughter as bright as the stars;
the tender embraces, the music and wine,
the minstrels with painted guitars.

But now I can see, as reality dawns,
he's sent in his place a young man ...
a son who has grown to look much as he did
on the day our adventure began.

Approaching me swiftly, he offers his hand.
"Saluti!" His voice is so deep.
He draws from his pocket a letter for me.
"Here's something you may want to keep."

I thank him and ask all the questions I can.
As he answers each one, I can see
he's charming and kind, much the same as my friend,
who regrets he can't be here with me.

I learn of an accident, hospital time --
a long, slow recovery too.
He tells me of things all those letters left out,
such as lovers that I never knew.

But nothing, I find, can displace what we'd shared,
or diminish the one I adore.
Perhaps, I discover, friendship is enough,
although my heart longed for much more.

The parting is sweet as we share a warm hug.
"Farewell," I say. "Ciao," he replies.
Again I'm transported to that tearful day
in the shade of the church. Sad goodbyes

are sometimes much more than they seem at the time,
much more than two friends ever dreamt.
Though one dreamed of love and the other of life,
both managed a lifetime well-spent.

Much later, I open the letter he sent
and read, through the blur of my tears,
regrets and apologies, love ever strong,
and a hope that endured through the years.

I stand in the shadows, alone once again.
Orvieto, the town of lost dreams,
now stretches below me in quiet repose.
The last of the evening sun gleams

like a heavenly blessing upon the old church
where I, long ago, pledged my heart.
I whisper "Addio" to unfulfilled dreams
but not to the joy dreams impart.

Goodbye to the beautiful town, Orvieto.
I doubt I will ever return,
but wonderful memories forever remain,
with some lessons I needed to learn.

Dissipating Steam

Steam rises from my coffee cup and fills the air with fragrance.
I sip and think of how you shared, with love and quiet patience,
when last I saw you at the lake that chilly winter evening.
As steamy mist rose eerily, you told me you were leaving.

I understood your reasoning and why you chose to go,
but still, the teardrops stung my eyes ... for much we'd never know.
There were so many memories cascading through my mind.
The words I sought remained unsaid, emotions undefined.

It was too difficult to say goodbye to one more dear
than any friend I'd ever known. I longed to keep you near.
But innocence and shyness joined together to impart
a calm acceptance that belied the aching in my heart.

As young and awkward children might, we struggled to convey
the deepness of the feelings shared before you went away.
The years passed by incessantly. I'd ask old friends about you,
but had to settle for a life devoid of love without you.

Now, as my scalding coffee hurts, like dreams superfluous,
I wonder how things might have been, had fate been true to us.
Today I read you'd gone away, but this time, no goodbye.
There'll be no meeting now for us, until I too shall die.

It is my hope, if we might meet on that celestial shore,
at last I'll find the words to say, "I should have loved you more."

An Unexpected Grace

He was my friend until the day he died,
and when his heart stopped, mine grew strangely still.
I thought my life had ended and I cried
for all the hopes and dreams we'd not fulfill.

The night was long and dark. I wept such tears
as I have never, ever shed before,
until at last I slept, to dream of years
that slipped away like breakers on the shore.

On waking, I was filled with sad regret
that never more I'd see his smiling face.
But like a song, his laughter lingers yet
within my heart, an unexpected grace ...

an undeserved but cherished gifting of
a quiet joy and never-ending love.

At Close of Day

Wind chimes
announce the breeze
whose steps we never hear,
and bless the evening air with sound
of song.

Tanka (hovering moon gleams)

hovering moon gleams
like a father's watchful eye
through the tree branches
recalcitrant meadowlark
sings love songs in the darkness

Blossoming

A newborn child
is like a tender flower ...
bright petals waiting to unfold
beneath love's gentle shower.

Butterfly Song

I will enfold you
in the silken threads of love
until your heart has wings.

Beautiful Lake Tahoe

Before the sunlight slips away, I sit,
Enjoying evening's peace upon the lake ...
A quiet time of introspection, dreams
Unrolling in the ribbons of soft light.
Tranquility prevails, as daylight fades,
Its cache of nagging troubles fading too,
For here, amidst such beauty, God is felt.
Unmindful of the time, I linger long,
Lest, in my haste, I somehow miss the moment.

Life whispers softly through the swaying pines
And echoes from the snowy mountain side.
Kindhearted night birds add their songs of cheer,
Each one a sweet reminder of God's love.

The night creeps in along the eastern ridge
And with the darkness comes a lifting breeze.
How beautifully the stars fill lake and sky ...
Omnipotent display of heaven's wealth,
Engendering in me a ceaseless awe.

My God and I

I.
While very young, I learned to talk with God
and in my heart I came to honor Him.
His beauty glowed, as by cool streams I trod.
I felt His presence in the forests dim.

The mountain skies proclaimed His majesty
as countless stars beamed brilliance from above,
and in a quiet lake as well, I'd see
the radiant reflection of His love.

But time brought changes I could not abide
and bitterness crept in to scar my heart
the day my closest friend, my brother, died.
How could a caring God rip us apart?

I'd trusted that my Lord's almighty hand
would keep him safe, and did not understand.

II.
To trust in God may seem a simple thing,
for everywhere we gaze, creation shines.
We find such beauty in the sighing pines
and in the warbles woodland sparrows sing.
Within the clear, sweet waters of a spring,
we sometimes hear the voice of the Divine;
these messages of love were always mine,
until one day the joy bells ceased to ring.

For pain and disappointment take their toll
and broken hearts may wander in distress,
away from One who makes the weakest strong.
And so it was, I found my weary soul
soon numb to God's great beauty and largess,
not knowing He was with me all along.

III.
A soul who walks in anger cannot see
the beauty of creation, nor God's plan
to bless His child with love abundantly ...
the love that lit the world since time began.

I drifted lost, a wounded, searching man,
unable to enjoy what should astound,
unable to perceive, as some men can,
the splendor of creation all around.

But somehow I was touched by Love profound
while glimpsing, from on high, a flawless lake.
As I, from my small plane, was gazing down,
I felt within my heart, a new dawn break.

At last I knew, the One who had made this,
could surely fill my cheerless heart with bliss.

IV.
Surrendering my broken, willful ways,
I asked Him to forgive my angry heart.
I vowed to honor God throughout my days,
if He would somehow make this rage depart.

I knew my brother would not want to see
the way I had been living, so adrift.
To Him who understood my misery,
I prayed at last, to feel this sadness lift.

At once the cockpit filled with glowing light.
The lake below reflected rainbow hues.
I knew I'd been transformed; my heart's delight
would ever be to tell this wondrous news.

Now, love and blessings overflow my soul,
and just to honor Him, is my life's goal.

After Rain

After rain, the leaves wear sequins on their silken gowns
and dance in circles to the music of the breeze.
After rain, the robins peek out from their lofty nests
and venture down to find new worms beneath the trees.

After storms, the dark clouds part to give the amber sun
a chance to light the world once more, or hang a bow
of multi-colored promises, which seems to say
God cares for us, and knows, through storms our faith will grow.

The Stars Don't Care

There is a reason for what comes our way.
There is a destiny that's purely ours;
but who can tell the impact when we pray
or know how much our future rests in stars?

I've lived too long to not believe in prayer.
My path is strewn with answers sent from God,
and though the stars are brilliant, they don't care
about my heart or where my feet have trod.

Love Endures

This evening, strolling barefoot in the sand,
I thought of weighted words you'd said to me
one summer as we walked beside the sea ...
kind words that only friends would understand
who shared a bond like ours, a golden strand
of loving trust and camaraderie.
You promised we'd be friends eternally.
There'd be no storm our love could not withstand.

I stopped and pondered everything you'd said
as sinking sun lit waves with burnished light.
I knew, deep in my heart, the path ahead
would sometimes lead through shadows, but the sight
of sunset painting sea and clouds with red
assured me sun-kissed love endures the night.

I've Only a Prayer

Here, on the outskirts of our little town,
the roadways are dark at night
and even the windows of homes around
will soon be devoid of light.

The moon shines brightly through ebony trees
and the stars are brighter too,
making the heavens seem closer to me,
drawing me nearer to you.

When I look up from my darkening place
under the sheltering skies,
in the moon I can see your smiling face,
in the stars, your winking eyes.

The breeze, gently brushing aside my hair,
is whispering in my ear,
telling me softly I mustn't despair,
reminding me you are near.

The sound of the trees as they bend and sigh,
is a melody in the night,
like a song to my heart from days gone by,
when life was warmer and bright ...

but here in the darkness, I've only a prayer
for your heart to know endless peace,
and a wish to be by your side, for there
the music will never cease.

A Light in the Darkness

When I was tempted to give up and cry,
your love appeared like sunlight through the rain.
Your smile brought hope that bowed across the sky
and made me glad to look up once again.

When I was lost in fear and so alone
and strangers lurked in every shadowed place,
your hand reached out to me and led me home
where love forgives and life is touched by grace.

When I was listening for a cheerful note
to brighten up a world devoid of song,
you knew exactly what I needed most
and sang the words that made me sing along.

When I looked for a gentle friend to care,
and make me laugh when all else made me sad,
I simply turned around and you were there,
and now my heart is full and I am glad.

When I am tempted to forget to say
how much your presence in my life has meant,
your gifts of love remind me every day
and even night becomes a bright event.

Where Wisdom Waits

When young, I often questioned
where true wisdom waits,
and why, when I inquire,
she coyly hesitates.

Perhaps I wouldn't know her
even if she came,
although I vainly seek her,
enamored of her name.

But after years of searching,
uncertain where to look,
I found her one day, waiting
inside God's Holy Book.

A Song for Father

He burst upon our morning like the sun,
and with his brightness, stirred our slumbering minds.
He walked with clouds where mountain rivers run,
and saw great vistas, - found what few men find.

His love and laughter filled our days with light
and taught us of a great, enduring Love
which flows beyond the boundaries of night
to reconcile the world to life above.

But, as the setting sun slips past the hill
and suddenly the warmth of day is gone,
so, when he died, the evening shadow's chill
was felt in every heart that knew him long.

Yet truth and wisdom, through a lifetime shared,
are passed along to young lives just begun.
New hope, new hearts arise from one that cared,
and morning after morning brings the sun.

True Dignity

True dignity describes itself
in simple, quiet ways.
A man of pride and principle
is not by truth dismayed.
Deep wisdom and integrity,
each act of his displays,
and never by temptation's call,
will his strong heart be swayed.

My Mother's Words

She had a quiet smile, a twinkling eye,
a loving touch that said, "I'm here... Don't cry."
She was a teacher who would lend a hand,
but with a heart that seemed to understand
the need for little ones to stand alone,
and feel as if they were already grown.

She taught me how to love without restraint
and how to suffer pain without complaint.
She modeled for me how to be a wife
and sought to honor God throughout her life.
At last, when time for her had reached its end,
I saw how thrilled she was to meet her Friend.

The days without her seemed too hard to bear,
and often I would wish she were still there;
but soon I came to recognize that she,
in many ways, was here, still guiding me.
The principles she taught would never leave,
and for that reason, I'd less cause to grieve …

for mother's words still shine like beacon lights
across the sea of years, through life's dark nights.

A Mother's Love

A mother's love
is like the silent sifting of
new snow through sleepy, starless night
that gently covers huddled hills
and trees and fills
the darkness with a holy light.

Izzy's Story (I Missed You Today)

"I missed you today, my Darling,"
I breathed, as the fresh evening breeze
ruffled across the clear water
and sang in the towering trees.

My heart is still aching without her,
the only love I've ever known.
But I'm taking the trip we had planned,
though it hurts to be traveling alone.

We shared such a passion for life.
She alone filled my every desire,
as we lovingly raised our two sons,
with big dreams for when I'd retire.

But sometimes we don't get our wishes.
I wish she were with me tonight,
at rest here beside the wide river
enjoying the lingering light.

Each night, in my camper's small bed,
I pray that somehow, in my dreams
she'll come and be near me once more.
That's all I have left now, it seems.

The evening shadows grow deeper.
But suddenly, there's a strange sound.
So, leaving my sad remembering,
I get up to go look around.

I discover inside my back window,
the flutter of silver-green wings.
It's a humming bird, gazing intently
as if with a message to bring.

Perhaps it is just from my longing,
and memories of what used to be,
but the tiny bird brings to my mind
the bird feeders on every tree

across our back yard where my sweetheart
so often would watch with delight
as the hummingbirds gathered for dinner
just at the sun's fading light.

My heart skips a beat at the memory ...
Such joy her small birds always brought,
so I linger, to taste one more second,
the sweetness this moment has wrought.

But I know I must help the small bird
get back to the wilds and the wood.
So, using my newspaper, gently
I show it the door, as I should.

"You've come to remind me of her,"
I whisper, not wanting to harm
or frighten the beautiful creature
who shows not a sign of alarm.

But then, to my utter amazement,
it slows in its fluttering flight
and hops on top of my paper,
then into my hand. What delight!

Convinced no one will believe this,
I reach, with my un-busy hand,
for my camera, preserving the sight
of this gift I cannot understand.

Then carefully, still disbelieving
the bird might remain for a while,
I capture forever, an image ...
a moment that made my heart smile.

Then, into the skies, winging swiftly,
my visitor leaves me. I'm blessed
by God's touch of infinite kindness
and grace, more than I'd ever guessed.

"I'll miss you forever, my Darling,"
I say as I watch the bird's flight.
"Though you've flown to a place I can't go,
I know you were with me tonight."

Pleasure Trip

I hear the rumble of the weighted years
as life rolls swiftly down the rails of time,
her dancing light and shade a pantomime
in rhythm with the rocking freight of tears.
Too soon she rounds the bend and disappears.
Far off, the children's mocking voices chime
a long-forgotten, haunting nursery rhyme,
while vivid in my memory appears

a little child at play, with waking heart
and eager mind in search of life, not knowing
the train arrives, so quickly to depart.
Now, as the singing wheels at last are slowing,
I recognize a truth I would impart ...
The pleasure is the ride, not where it's going.

Step by Step

My life is like a stairway
with several flights to climb,
and every segment traveled
leads through a different time.

The first flight is my childhood
where steps are very small
and pass through golden gardens
enclosed behind a wall.

There, sunlight filters warmly
through shady boughs of care
that shelter and protect me
from harshness and despair.

The days are filled with laughter
and music is a part
of happy, easy hours,
as love enfolds my heart.

But time compels me onward
to life beyond the wall,
into a world of duties
with steps no longer small.

With ease I learn to climb them,
for I am larger too,
and anxious to be "grown up"
with grander things to do.

Traversing youth, my staircase
takes many twists and turns,
a spiral climb that takes me
to where new passion burns,

and where, when day is over,
soft moonlight makes me feel
as if the world I live in
is magically surreal.

But soon the steps grow steeper
and difficult to climb,
for here I am protector
of other lives than mine.

I watch with awe and wonder
as little ones begin
the steps I know will take them
to where I've never been.

At last my steps have brought me
onto a landing where
I've time to look around me
and breathe sweet autumn air.

As life moves swiftly forward,
more difficult the climb,
until that final stair step ...
the pinnacle of time.

It's then I will surrender
to what God has in store,
and with His hand to guide me,
I'll step on Heaven's shore.

A Touch of Heaven

I hold you close, so still and small and sweet,
asleep against my waiting breasts,
and I am filled with wonder. I am awed
to think of all the hopes, the wealth of dreams,
the wide expanse of life that rests
within this little package sent from God.

To be a mother makes my life complete.
My precious baby, perfect gift of love,
you are more loved than you will ever know.
I kiss your nose and feel your tiny hand
surround my finger like a glove,
and know a touch of heaven here below.

Children on my Knees

I held my children close and watched them grow,
and prayed all heaven be theirs while here below.
Each day their tiny steps brought new delight,
and love sustained through every troubled night.

But soon they grew beyond the bounds of home
to find the world stretched wider than they'd known.
Their larger steps were anxious now to stray
in search of life and growth along the way.

Though love cried out in fear, I could not reach
to hold them back from all that life would teach,
but prayed, with tears, I'd done the best I could
to help them honor right and choose the good.

But now, surrounded by my memories
of times I held them laughing, on my knees,
I hold then yet, though they are unaware,
as on my knees, I hold them up in prayer.

To Taste the Rain

Intently she bends to touch the window,
her small hands pressed against the icy pane,
her young eyes glistening in anticipation ...
listening to the drumming of the rain.

Gently now, she smiles, her dimpled face
mirrored in the glass, so like my own,
reminding me how swiftly winters pass,
how soon our sense of wonder is outgrown.

Eventually she turns and finds my eyes
brimming with the love I can't contain,
and knowing I am helpless to refuse,
she tugs me toward the door to taste the rain.

Relentlessly we run, her hatless head
turned up, the dampness shining on her face;
the warmth of her small hand in mine, a gift
my heart will hold and time cannot erase.

Heart Play

Like clouds aloft, the years fly past.
The child can't last,
except, I find,
within my mind.

Though wrinkles crease my laughing eyes,
this satisfies:
my heart still plays
in yesterdays ...

for poets, with fresh wonder, see
what life can be,
and fill each line
with warm sunshine.

Face in the Mirror

I stand before my mirror
and see, to my surprise,
my mother looking back at me
with mischief in her eyes.

"What happened, Mom?" I ask her.
"How did I get your face?
Who took away your baby girl
and put you in her place?"

My mother grins and twinkles
the way she used to do.
"I guess you didn't listen when
I said this would be true!

"The child you were still lives there
inside your poet's heart.
Your face has changed but there remains
an awe that won't depart."

I see the teardrops glisten
in mother's thought-filled eyes,
and feel my own eyes sting with tears.
That's when I realize

the face is *not* my mother's,
though similar I know.
The years have passed. Now, in the glass,
my age begins to show.

But in my heart there dances
a child, a dream-filled lass,
who looks at life through wonder's eyes,
not in a looking glass.

Bird Words

The other day, I went downtown
and stumbled on the strangest scene.
I stepped into a darkened bar,
compelled by thirst. Know what I mean?

The searing heat of afternoon
had parched my throat and left me beat,
so, thought I'd have a cooling drink,
relax a bit, get off my feet.

I quickly found a quiet spot,
a little table near the back
where I could be alone to think
and drink and have a little snack.

I hadn't been there very long
before I saw, to my surprise,
the guy behind the bar had wings,
a beak and two black, beady eyes.

As if that were not bad enough,
I noticed then, on every stool,
that only birds had bellied up,
all sipping drinks and acting cool.

I saw a dark, distinguished one,
though slightly bald, a regal eagle,
chatting up a gal in white ...
I'm pretty sure she was a seagull.

On two adjacent stools, I saw
a pair of penguins dressed to kill
in black tuxedos, drinking wine
and being careful not to spill.

A pelican with under-bite
seemed slightly sad, but nursed a drink
while next to him, his feathered friend
kept flaunting her flamingo pink.

The barkeep sauntered over then,
and in a language strange to me,
said something cold that made me feel
he didn't like my company.

I looked around for just one friend,
afraid to smile or even grin,
because, in bird bars, I could see
no one had lips. Might be a sin

to let my happy nature show.
So, nervously, afraid to laugh,
I turned my head away and vowed
to stifle mirth on their behalf.

That's when I saw, to my surprise,
a parrot sweeping up some wheat.
With feathers ruffled, much like mine,
he used some words I can't repeat,

but such relief came over me
as finally I understood
how, even in a bird-brained world,
a common language feels so good!

He Cares Not

A seagull stepped across the mirrored sands
and left his tiny hieroglyphics there;
but in the night, the sea, with silver hands,
erased the prints the gull made without care.

A poet wrote with fervor through the years
and left impassioned words on every page,
not knowing, as he spilled his love and tears,
who might in time, consider him a sage,

or who, among his readers, might decide
his metaphors were meaningless, his words
as worthless as the gull's prints. Would time's tide
erase them as if markings left by birds,

or might they shine throughout eternity?
He cares not which; he *must* write poetry.

What Makes You Write?

"What makes you write?" my sister asked.
I had a ready answer.
"Just show me words; there lies my task.
As music moves a dancer,

so words sing melodies to me,
and make my heart beat faster.
Their rhythmic pulse speaks poetry.
I am both slave and master."

My sister stared with widened eyes,
her lips so sweetly pursed.
"Your answer fills me with surprise.
I've thought you might be cursed!"

"Ah, cursed indeed," I answered then,
"and blessed as well, it seems,
for words possess me, move my pen
and fill my mind with dreams."

As much as I loved words, I found
I scarce could make her see
how words are friends. They sing and sound
like symphonies to me.

As you can see, I don't speak well,
for shyness makes me quiet,
but poetry has cast its spell.
I am compelled to try it.

"I'll write it out for you," I said.
"Explaining takes much time."
With words like dancers in my head,
I wrote this little rhyme.

Sisters on the Step

It seems like only yesterday we sat here,
children on the peeling step,
a tin of soggy soap between us,
blowing bubbles from the ends of empty spools.

We'd watch with wonder as each limpid globe
would grow and stretch around our silent breath,
reflecting rainbow-tinted images of porch and trees
and faces soft with innocent delight.

Before the bubbles burst, we'd fling them free
and gasp to see them soar and shimmer in the sun,
or laugh when they would bump together, quaking,
sometimes breaking in a soapy splash.

But now and then a sturdy one
would catch the breeze and seem to soar
beyond the tangled branches of the trees,
or even, we imagined, on beyond the mountain peaks
where we could only dream of going.

Like bright clouds skidding swiftly on a windswept sky,
the years have flown, and now, once more
we sit here on the shadowed step,
fond sisters sharing thoughts and dreams
that breathe from deep within.

Reflective, touched by rainbow lights,
they glow with hope and tug our hearts together,
making laughter splash and overflow.

But dreams, we find, sometimes soar higher
than our hearts can follow ... far beyond
the tangled reaches of our lives,
beyond the clouds that shroud the mountain peaks,
and on to that elusive place where only dreams can go.

A Sister's Smile

There is a special bond that sisters share,
a warm togetherness unique and strong.
No matter what, you know she's always there,
assuring you she'll fix whatever's wrong.

A sister knows the pathways you have traveled,
the valleys and the mountain tops you've viewed.
She's gathered up the threads when dreams unraveled
and helped you start again with hopes renewed.

There is no gift from God's abundant store
that can surpass the gift of sisterhood.
But when you turn, and find she's there no more,
you cling with love, to mem'ries kind and good,

and thank the Lord above, who for a while,
allowed you to enjoy a sister's smile.

A Private Word With My Father

I cannot help but think of you today,
as morning rays of sun slant through the trees.
In memory's waking light, I watch you pray
beside the window, Bible on your knees,

eyes filled with tears of reverence as you gaze
across the lake to distant mountain range.
The silent waters, shrouded in soft haze,
await the breezes' touch to bring them change,

just as you wait in silence for the touch
of God's sweet spirit on your thirsting soul.
The years of work and struggle taught you much,
but perfect bliss was never your life's goal ...

Instead you sought to bring true joy to others,
to tell them of the One who seeks to save,
whose endless mercy offers love that covers,
transforming lives once destined for sin's grave.

Your calloused hands rest on the well-worn book.
Your eyes take in the tranquil mountain scene
as I, observing from my quiet nook,
thank God for home and all contentment means.

Though many are the years, and quickly flown,
since childhood's peaceful days of innocence,
I'll be forever grateful to have known
your giving heart, so gentle, so immense.

The lessons you imparted guide me still.
The mem'ries of your life, like scrolls unfurled,
became my dreams ... my purpose to fulfill ...
with love that flows beyond this mortal world.

At Evening

The evening sun sends rays of lazy light
obliquely filtered through the distant trees,
to cast long shadows that portend the night
and stir my heart to search old memories.

The dreams of youth, like daylight, fade away,
but somehow send warm thoughts of tender years
to filter through the branches of my day
and light my path before the night appears.

My weary thoughts turn toward my distant home
and those whose love surrounded me with light;
a love unlike all others I have known,
and faith dispelling any fear of night.

Home at Last

Somewhere in a quiet meadow, rests a stately, waiting home.
Tall trees shade the grassy lawn where deer and wild things freely roam.
Morning sun ignites the windows with its radiant, flame-like glow
and awakes a sleeping mother, aging now, with movements slow.

She will rise and make the coffee, feed the cat and light the fire,
then, with Bible opened, offer prayers for her heart's desire.
Years have passed since her loved daughter wandered off into the night.
Every morning finds her pleading God would keep her child in sight,

fill her heart with peace and goodness, let her know her mother's love
never falters in its power, but, like sunlight from above,
will be ever strong and steadfast, even though her child be lost,
always hopeful, always loving, never mindful of the cost.

When the sun has ceased its journey through the heavens toward the west,
and before the golden moonlight gently shines upon her rest,
mother and her kitten settle near the fire to watch it burn,
as another prayer is lifted for her daughter's safe return.

Thus the years move slowly onward. Every day remains the same.
Sun shines on a mother praying; evening breezes speak the name
of the one so loved and cherished, never far from heart or mind.
Then, one midnight, in her slumbers, mother leaves her grief behind,

rising to her Master's homeland where there is no need for sun.
All the weariness has left her. Now, at last, the battle's won.
She's assured her heart's petition will become reality,
and the child so dearly loved, will meet her in eternity.

~ ~ ~ ~ ~ ~

Somewhere in a quiet meadow rests a stately, silent home.
Tall trees shade the grassy lawn, where deer and wild things freely
roam.
In the kitchen, by the window where the sun's warm rays are cast,
stands the daughter, softly weeping, grateful to be home at last.

I've Loved You Fiercely

I.
I've loved you fiercely since I first beheld
your tiny hands and feet, your clear, blue eyes.
Such overwhelming love your face compelled!
I wept with joy to hear your newborn cries.

I watched you grow into a child so sweet,
I thought at first, it was an angel born
into my world ... a world now made complete
by Heaven's kiss, that sunny, summer morn.

But winter took away your sun-bright smile
and left a chilling weight of ice and snow.
My aching heart sought ways to reconcile
the change, and asked, where did my angel go?

However, as December heralds May,
I was so sure you would return some day.

II.
I was so sure you would return some day,
I gladly left the porch light on each night,
and every morning, kneeling down to pray,
I asked the Lord to guide your steps aright.

Although I may not know just where you are,
you can be found within my yearning heart.
I see you in the soft light of a star
and hear you in the music birds impart.

But you must know how much I long to feel
your kiss upon my cheek, your loving touch.
It seems no words can ever quite reveal
a mother's longing when she's lost so much.

This Mother's Day, I pray you'll hear my heart ...
I've loved you fiercely from the very start.

Time's Attire

The Past slips wearily away
along the pathways of my mind.
Her faded garments, memories,
are carelessly cast off behind.
I gather them and find them kind.

The Present churns and whirls about,
so frantically I scarce can see
the colors of her patterned gown,
or grasp the choreography,
and yet her music beckons me.

With thread-bare thoughts and misty-eyed,
I look ahead, where Hope, it seems,
is nursing Future at her breast,
wrapped tenderly in wispy dreams,
soft dreams that only time redeems.

Reflecting

I see a crystal mountain lake
as blue as any sky,
surrounded by a stand of pines,
and loving it, I sigh.

Reflected in its mirrored blue
I see the girl I was,
a happy child who loved her life,
forgetful of its flaws.

I hear the gentle slap of waves
against the neighbor's pier,
as morning winds begin to sigh
across the waters near.

I see the girl dive in and swim
through icy depths with ease
until the coldness numbs her and
she pauses, just to breathe.

She floats in quiet solitude,
and in the silence, seems
to find a peace no other place
can offer. Here she dreams

of life beyond this azure lake,
and golden dawns to come.
Then, as the sun climbs up the sky,
she swims, no longer numb.

I see her flashing arms of bronze
now pulling for the shore
and suddenly my heart is moved
by all that went before.

Nostalgia mingles pleasantly
with what has come to pass.
The person that I used to be,
that happy, carefree lass,

is still a part of who I am,
though now maturity
disguises and transforms somehow
the old reality.

I stand beside my mountain lake.
The swimmer reaches land,
emerging as a woman now.
I smile and take her hand.

Boundless Love

There is a love that knows no boundaries,
a love which flows from an eternal source
and hums around the heart like honeybees.
Such is the love I hold, a whelming force.
Since you have filled my life with all things sweet
and poured your tender heart out at my feet,
I walk on mountain peaks where angels greet.

I see you here beside me, curled in sleep,
the comforter tucked 'round your snuggled chin,
and as you slumber, I must try to keep
myself from smoothing out your hair, grown thin
and white with nature's unrelenting years,
yet beautiful to me. What disappears
from sight remains in recollection's spheres.

Now, memories wash over me once more,
much like the sudden sweep of ocean waves
might rush upon sunbathers on the shore,
and I am stunned at how my heart behaves
when flooded by remembrances of you ...
those sacred moments, special things we'd do
as day by day, the love between us grew.

My heart is filled, as if from mountain springs,
with such a flood of love, so clear and pure,
and while the child in me would dance and sing,
in deference to my age, I act demure,
and only smile as songs rise silently,
in honor of the joy o'erfilling me ...
a joy that grows in its intensity.

I've known this love that has no boundaries
and surely flows from an eternal source.
Though sweet as honey, strong as throbbing seas
is this unfailing love my heart outpours.
You murmur in your sleep. I take your hand
and kiss it softly. This hand, strong and tanned,
was meant for me ... a marriage God had planned.

But I Don't Know

If there was not an ocean, wide and deep,
if there were not so many sparkling stars,
if there were not sweet dreams each time I sleep,
I then, perhaps could doubt this love of ours.

If babies never cooed at mother's smile,
if poets never spoke of love as real,
if thoughts of you were absent for a while,
perhaps I could deny the way I feel.

If earth might stop, and sun refuse to rise,
if wind chimes failed to sing when breezes blow,
if you could quench the love-light in your eyes,
then maybe I could too ... but I don't know.

Precious Time

The night we met, it seemed all time stood still.
We danced to music only we could hear,
as moonlight cast our shadows on the hill.
You walked me home, then whispered in my ear,

"I'll love you for as long as I have breath.
I can't imagine life without you in it."
And I replied, "I'll love you until death ...
each day and night and every precious minute."

The years flew by as if in phantom dreams,
but love grew stronger with each fleeting day.
Our time ran out before our love, it seems,
for on a starless night, you slipped away.

Death would not wait. It tore our worlds apart,
but time can't steal the love that fills my heart.

When Love Is Born

When strangers meet and love is born,
the stars all clap their hands in glee
and moonbeams, like bright jewels, adorn
the crowns of heaven's royalty.

When love becomes a growing child
that's nurtured gently until strong,
the sun shines warmly, seas are wild
with melodies of circling song.

When love matures and blooms anew,
the orchards blossom with fresh seed
as every tree rejoices too
in reproduction's potent need.

When love is born and love survives,
it is because two lovers cared,
for with such care, the seedling thrives
and multiplies, if love is shared.

Strange Liberty

You promised you would never leave.
It was so easy to believe,
because your eyes revealed love in your heart.
But suddenly you were not there.
I searched and wept and in despair,
accepted we must live our lives apart.

The silence, like a thunder, boomed.
My world was shaken, our love doomed.
Too often in the night, I woke with tears.
But once, I dreamed you took my hand
and tried to help me understand
how life goes on and changes come with years.

Then, in the darkness, for a time
I felt your heart beat next to mine,
as if we were as we had always been.
But when I woke, I realized
you'd been my dream, idealized,
and found new strength to rise, begin again ...

For life is not a perfect dream
and rarely are things as they seem,
yet dreams can sometimes set the wounded free.
In memory, I hold you still
and know perhaps I always will,
with gratitude for love's strange liberty.

Shipwrecked

I pledged my heart and soul to you
and sealed it with a sacred vow.
You gave me shelter from the storms,
but where is my safe harbor now?

I thought you loved as I love you.
We sailed life's vessel without fear
through turbulent or gentle seas.
Where are you now, my love so dear?

You gave no sign of mutiny ...
no shots were fired across the bow.
One day I turned and you were gone.
Oh where is my safe harbor now?

I weep for you with broken heart.
The sea can't hold another tear.
You were my anchor and my port.
Where are you now, my love so dear?

Without You

Seagulls circle endlessly above the cliffs,
their lonely cry an echo in my heart.
I think of all the happy times I've spent with you
and how it hurts to have to be apart.

With broken shells, I sit here idly drawing
empty hearts, small symbols in the sand,
then watch the waves rush in to wash them all away,
and wonder if I'll ever understand.

The sinking sun slips silently behind the clouds,
and while the darkness shrouds the shore with peace,
I count the stars the way I'll count the nights until
your arms around me make this aching cease.

This Dreary Place

The morning dawns with laziness,
the sun reluctant to be seen.
A dreary fog, a haziness,
surrounds me like an eerie dream

as wearily I creep from bed,
my limbs as heavy as my heart,
and stumble down the hall with dread,
to face, as now I must, the start

of this new life, the empty days
without the pleasure of your voice,
no words to warm or offer praise,
no reasons now to smile, rejoice.

Too early, the night's slumbers fled,
and left me counting memories.
Too many were the tears I'd shed
in supplication on my knees.

But God, who sees each sparrow's pain,
must surely see this broken heart.
Without His love, no love remains
to guide me now that we're apart.

I fill the coffee pot and turn
to see the struggling sun appear.
Somehow I sense my heart will learn
to smile without your presence near.

The smell of coffee comforts me.
It's such a little thing, I know,
but step by step, eventually,
I'll learn to live and let you go.

The morning sun in gentle rays
creeps in and fills this dreary place.
I hold my warming cup and pray
I'll find at last, God's healing grace.

Memories and Dreams

Where mem'ries play and dreams come true,
in forests green beside the lake,
that's where I want to stay with you.
Such magic our two hearts will make.

In forests green beside the lake
while watching golden sun arise,
such magic our two hearts will make
beneath the glow of mountain skies.

While watching golden sun arise,
we'll speak of love and other things
beneath the glow of mountain skies,
as geese and swallows spread their wings.

We'll speak of love and other things,
embraced by shadows from the trees.
As geese and swallows spread their wings,
lake waters ripple in the breeze.

Embraced by shadows from the trees,
that's where I want to stay with you.
Lake waters ripple in the breeze
where mem'ries play and dreams come true.

Drifting Memories

When summer heat burned through the fog of youth
and seared the tender sapling's budding leaves,
I searched the shoreline for a grain of truth
to nourish dreams an innocent perceives.

When autumn turned the trees to burnished gold
and youth had changed her garments for life's dance,
I traveled yet again the paths we strolled,
the shaded trails where once we found romance.

But now that winter's come and you are gone,
I taste the snow upon my thirsting tongue,
and long to feel the warmth of summer's dawn
and know the star-filled nights that thrill the young.

I watch the tender snowflakes drifting past
like memories, and pray a few will last.

Night Gives Way

The night's soft rain subsides before the dawn
and leaves the air and grasses sweet and clean.
The waking sun sends light to paint the clouds
in shifting shades of peach and yellow-gold.

I smell the roses' elegant perfume
and watch the daffodils and iris sway
as if they hear the music in the wind,
a whispered call to join in nature's dance.

Soft memories of you rise in the mist ...
We too once moved to melodies unheard
by anyone but us, as arm in arm,
we waltzed in time to love's unfailing beat.

You were the fragrance in each quiet dawn
and stirred my senses to awake with zest,
yet through the darkest night, your presence brought
a consolation you alone could give.

It is no wonder that I miss you so
and long to hold you close in love's embrace,
but if, on Heaven's shore, there is a breeze,
perhaps it lifts to you my heart's desire.

I pray you'll know why I no longer dance
since angels took you home and left me here.
Still, in the morning sun I see your smile
and pain abates, like showers in the night.

Wistful Smiles

The moon, a silver sliver in the sky,
is curved into what seems a wistful smile.
I wonder if you see it too, and sigh
to think of every long and lonely mile

we've traveled since you left so long ago.
I wonder if your smile is wistful too,
and do you wish, as stars begin to glow,
that I might once again be there with you?

A wisp of cloud appears and, like a veil
a widow wears in mourning, hides the moon.
The smile is gone as memories grow pale
and hope as well, is fading in the gloom.

But clouds and time move on and soon, I'd guess,
once wistful smiles will glow with happiness.

Silver Moon

A slice of silver moon
sails high across the sky,
though neither sails nor current,
assist her passing by.

The morning, like a mist,
obscures the light she wore;
but still she creeps, a ghost ship,
along horizon's shore.

Without Purpose

As honey bees without a meadow flower,
or dew without the sunlight's sparkling shine ...
as night without the stars, is empty darkness,
so is my heart, if you cannot be mine.

As melodies without a note to hold them,
must wander, pathless, through the realms of space,
so is my heart devoid of life's sweet music,
without your arms around in strong embrace.

As time is lost without day's boundaries
of moon's ascension and the setting sun,
my heart, as well, is lost without your love
and has no purpose once the day's begun.

Too Soon, You Rose

Out on the lawn, we sat in canvas chairs
and watched the sinking sun wink through the trees,
its colors warm, as was the love we shared,
in spite of autumn's chillness in the breeze.

As darkness crept across the dewy lawn
and shadows hid the smile within your eyes,
I reached to touch your hand, and heard a song.
Soft music filled the night with sweet surprise.

Your voice rose gently, singing heartfelt praise
to God whose love and caring meant so much.
I soon joined in, with gratitude for grace
and for the quiet blessing of love's touch.

With fingers linked, we sang in harmony
and felt the bond of joy true friendship brings.
Too soon, you rose and said goodbye to me,
and though I grieve, I know my heart still sings.

As cold and darkness linger for a while
and shadows hide your place out on the lawn,
I'll hold onto the love that lit your smile,
and greet you once again some Son-lit dawn.

Amazingly

Amazingly the path that was my life
has turned into an alley dark with pain.
The one who held my hand and led the way
is gone. No hope nor joy remains.

Amazingly, the world continues on
although my heart's companion slipped away.
To me it seems the sun no longer shines,
for in his smile I found the light of day.

Amazingly, the waves dance on the shore
and seagulls circle, playing overhead.
I feel as if all dancing should have ceased
for someone I have loved is lying dead.

Amazingly, I've found true love lives on
although the one who's loved may fade and die.
I cling to love as if it were a raft
adrift upon the tears I've learned to cry.

A Cup of Time

A cup of time was measured out for me
and when it was my turn, placed in my hand.
"It's all you'll get, so spend it carefully,"
He said, but knew I wouldn't understand.

A cup of time felt like a century.
I scattered drops and drank without concern.
A child's mind measures life so differently
and never dreams how much it has to learn.

The drops of time which once had filled my cup,
soon disappeared and left me wondering
what I had done. How had I used them up
and what had been achieved, if anything?

A cup of time is all each soul is spared.
The taste is sweeter when the cup is shared.

A Love I Never Knew

I wonder if there's ever been a time
when men did not create in cadenced beat,
and carefully contrive in flowing rhyme,
small songs of love in verses warm and sweet.

I wonder if there's ever been a spring
to spill its beauty over every hill
without some minstrel finding songs to sing ...
such songs as cause a maiden's heart to thrill.

I wonder if you'll know this song's for you
because my poet's heart encountered spring
and found within, a love I never knew.
Like meadowlarks, such love is born to sing.

At last I give it words and set it free
to soar to you on wings of poetry.

I Sometimes Wish

I sometimes wish the earth were not so round,
or that the sky could somehow be less blue.
But more, I wish this love my heart has found
could be the only love you ever knew.

I sometimes wish the love you blindly spurn
could fill you like the stars fill up the sky.
But still, unless the earth should cease to turn,
you'll never see the love that flows nearby.

I sometimes wish the one you hold so dear,
were not as beautiful as sunrise is,
or that the loving arms which pull her near,
could be around me, sharing Heaven's kiss,

But when the earth is flat and love lies cold
upon the ashes of my passion's fire,
perhaps you'll understand, this tale I've told
is of a love beyond this world's desire.

The love which melts my soul and fills my days
with hope for what I know can never be,
is burning like the sun through morning haze.
I sometimes wish your heart had eyes to see.

Starlight Love

A ghost wind moves across the yard tonight
and lifts the arms of my sequoia tree,
who waves her piney branches at the moon.
His golden face smiles back mysteriously.

I count the winking eyes of distant stars
which, like my own, can find no way to sleep,
and when, along the Milky Way, I'm lost,
I ponder love, unfathomably deep.

I've loved you since you galloped like the wind
across my yard, astride your ghost-white horse.
I've loved your golden smile, your winking eyes,
and how you lift my mind with your discourse.

Tonight I count the lights that marked our days,
flung wide like stars across the midnight skies,
and know I've loved each moment spent with you.
Such love will shine until the last star dies.

Endless Devotion

You are the fathomless ocean to me,
ever washing the sands of my days
with circling tides of sweet mystery,
and desire, like bonfires ablaze.

Into your depths I would willingly flow
like a river deep-swollen with rain,
till all that we are becomes one and I know
there is nothing can part us again.

You are the Milky Way lighting my night
with your wisdom ... a heavenly glow
affording me guidance and gentle insight
when I'm lost or unsure where to go.

You are my life, every day, every year.
You're my world, endless sky and deep ocean,
and I will be yours till the stars disappear ...
all I am, wrapped in endless devotion.

Love's Symphonies

As wind across the slumbering sea,
might stir its foam to frothy white,
so it is with you and me ...
you stir my slumbering soul tonight.

As rain fills up the mountain streams
and wakes the budding leaves of trees,
so it is, you fill my dreams,
and wake me with love's symphonies.

Just as the breaking rays of sun
dismiss the night and warm the earth,
so it is, you are the one
who satisfies my spirit's dearth.

A Natural Love

The tender snows enfold the distant hills.
The waves caress the shore with whispered song.
The trees bend gently to the wind's embrace
and moonlight's golden kisses fill the sky.

All nature sings of love, and my heart thrills.
It is no wonder then, that I might long
to hold you close and kiss your blissful face
and share with you this love I can't deny.

I Love Kisses

I love to walk along the sandy shore
and feel the kiss of ocean's misty spray.
But there are kisses I love even more …
the kisses you deliver every day.

I love to ride my gelding through the hills
and feel the kiss of breezes on my face,
but nothing equals all the shivered thrills
of sharing kisses locked in your embrace.

I love the kiss of moonlight on the lake,
a million stars reflected in each wave,
but lovely as it is, I wouldn't take
a billion for the kisses I most crave.

I love the kiss of rain on daffodils.
To see them nod their heads in sweet assent
reminds me how your gentle kiss now fills
my heart with endless love as yet unspent.

I love your kisses almost more than air,
and yes, you often take my breath away,
but there's no kiss on earth that can compare
to those you give me every night and day.

Castles by the Sea

Time at the sea ignites my blissful fuse.
A sunset just beyond the ocean's rim,
the quiet waves awash in golden hues,
bring memories that lift my thoughts to Him.
White seagulls soaring in majestic flight,
remind me yet, how God does all things right.

To watch a little child in simple play ...
sandcastles built with bridge and parapet,
bring happy thoughts of youth, another day,
a different child. My heart cannot forget
how mother's words would soothe away the frown,
when waves crashed in and knocked my castles down.

So many treasured memories surround
the ocean with its stretch of glistening beach ...
we children jumping rope with seaweed found
as tides receded, leaving it in reach,
or gathering unbroken star-shaped shells,
then dashing, carefree, into salty swells.

Sometimes, as stars appeared and moonlight shone,
we'd sit on sandy towels and sing a song
and often, other folks we hadn't known
would ask to join our fun and sing along.
These are the scenes, the memories that bless
and fill my heart with endless happiness.

I Met a Boy

I met a little boy one day,
so beautiful in every way;
my heart was stirred, although I knew not why.

His hair was fair, his eyes shone bright
with gentleness and love's soft light.
He took my hand and told me with a sigh,

"Someday I hope to be a king
and have a lot of everything,
so that no child would ever starve and die."

I saw at once he was sincere
and knowing that, I felt a tear
that could not be restrained, slip from my eye.

His smile was warm, his heart was pure.
How could such gentleness endure
the onslaught of this troubled world of pain?

I prayed he'd never have to see
how ugly this old world could be.
For him, I asked pure sunshine without rain,

for such a tender, loving soul
should not be thwarted from his goal
of giving, though it seemed I'd pray in vain.

All children lose their innocence
I thought, while hatred so immense
is bent upon destroying love's small gain.

I kissed my little friend goodbye
and saw a gleaming in his eye
that moved me in a way I'd never known.

Long, long years later by the sea,
I met a man who smiled at me
and in his eyes that same strange gleaming shone.

He sat beside me on the beach
and spoke of things beyond my reach.
At last I saw it was the boy, now grown.

In awe, I listened as he told
of love and truth. His words were bold
and seeds of hope within my heart were sown.

As day grew dim and stars appeared,
I somehow knew that what I'd feared
concerning how life's pain might rob the boy

of grace and love and ruin the soul
who yearned to see all children whole,
was not to be. This world could *not* destroy

the light that shone inside this one
whose zeal burned brighter than the sun,
whose every word welled up with love and joy,

as if, though life might be unkind,
he'd vowed to never leave behind
the wonder that had filled him as a boy.

At last he rose and took my hand
and drew me up that I might stand
beside him as we gazed across the sea.

I knew I'd met a man that day,
still beautiful in every way,
as full of love as any man could be,

a man who would not yield or bend
to anything that might offend
his gentle heart, his calm tranquility.

His eyes smiled warmly into mine
and brought a touch of love divine,
as he returned my hug so tenderly.

The endless ocean lapped the shore
and stars shone down just as before,
but something now had changed inside of me.

New hope was born afresh that night.
I sensed the world would be all right,
for in the end, Love gains the victory.

This gentle boy inside a man
had proved that wonder somehow can
survive the din of life's cacophony.

And though we never met again,
I found in him a timeless friend,
a friend I knew I'd love eternally.

Loneliness

Light fades and evening breezes softly stir.
Old mem'ries, like a whiff of fragrance, rise.
Nostalgic, I remember how things were ...
Embracing as we kissed beneath soft skies.

Love held us close; now love must let you go.
I'll always miss your touch, your special glow,
Not knowing how you are, or if you'll know

Each night I pause to watch the dimming sun
Slip down the sky, like hopes and dreams undone,
Still longing for its warmth, and yours, dear one.

Skies Aglow

Across the sky there sweeps a crimson glow,
as flowers fold to wait for morning dew
and quiet settles on the world below.
It's then my restless thoughts return to you.

Too long we've been apart; too wide the miles
that separate our hearts, our touch, our lives.
So difficult this road, these senseless trials.
Too many are the tears, yet faith survives.

The whisper of the trees salutes the night.
As breezes touch each gently nodding bloom,
I wait to dream, for dreams make all things right
and love surrounds like hyacinth perfume.

When morning comes, my waking hope will rise
to greet the glow across the eastern skies.

Sky Painting

An unseen hand paints rose and peach across the evening sky,
as wisps of clouds just out of reach, like daydreams, wander by.

I hear a gentle lullaby, the song the water sings,
while breezes stir and pines reply and night owls spread their wings.

Here, in the quiet of the night, my heart is singing too,
as images of days once bright, arise and hope shines through.

It's then I see the rose and peach as symbols of new joys,
and dreams that once seemed out of reach are dreams my heart employs

to paint the slowly darkening sky with laughter and with song ...
a time for love and poetry and friendships ever strong.

A Letter

Tears dampen lashes as I read
your love-laced poetry ...
sweet words that touch my waiting heart,
words written just for me.

Tears roll unchecked as I recall
the happy times we've shared
and lively conversations launched
like kites upon the air.

Tears turn to smiles as memories
remind me you are here
in all the words you send, to bring
your warmth and kindness near.

All doubts are banished, tears are dried.
A letter never fails
to bring fresh hope and happiness
when loneliness assails.

The Rock

I walked barefoot across the greening pasture,
the dampness of the grass bathing my soles.

A great loneliness loomed like a solitary tree
in the center of the sprawling meadow.

The rays of rising sun shone across the field
and cast a long shadow from the lonely tree.

I felt the chill on my back
where the shade touched me
and gathered my shawl closer about my shoulders.

Stooping, I scooped the dew
from the blades of meadow grass,
seeking to quench my thirst,
but to no avail.

Where I was going, I could not know,
but I walked and wondered until at last,
I saw the sun slip down the western sky
and turn the wispy clouds from gray to golden bronze.

My heart, as bare and cold as the feet beneath me,
embraced the gathering darkness,
welcoming the solitude of night.

The sharp, bright notes of a songbird
pierced the stillness
and I stopped to listen.

Turning, I saw a rock looming large
at the meadow's edge.
I approached, in search of a resting place.

As I leaned into its strength,
I felt the sun's lingering warmth
flow gently through me
like a healing touch.

There, on its solid shoulder, I lay like a weary child
until the morning came,
and a still, small voice
reminded me I had a Friend.

The Night Was Long

The night was long. No starlight shone,
no moon to smile a little while
for sleepless ones and those alone,
without a friend to call their own.

Dark clouds obscured the midnight sky
like hovered fears, then raindrop tears
washed unexpectedly, and I
as suddenly, began to cry.

The night seemed endless, but I knew
eventually, my grief would see
the warmth of morning sun shine through
to turn the cloud-dark skies to blue.

Believing this, at last I dozed.
The tears I'd cried, in dreams were dried
and when I woke, my heart arose
to greet the dawn where sunlight glows.

My window filled with morning light.
A robin's song rose from the lawn
and I was certain, through the night
God's love had worked to make things right.

Winter Waltz

A barren tree lays lacy limbs
in silhouette against the backlit sky
where clouds, like liquid mountains,
glide in silent waltz across the heavens,
billowing white skirts whirling
in and out of shadows.

Winter sun, as if an afterthought,
sends pale rays across the silvered scene,
sprinkling pristine snow
with glistening crystals.

Hand in hand, we walk the narrow road,
feet crunching in rhythmic beat
to winter's unique music,
hearts waltzing with the clouds,
moved by the beauty of
God's sunlit painting.

Winter Waiting

Bright Autumn occupies the stage,
her bawdy act a sight to see
as colors flash and trees are stripped
of each last leaf of dignity.

But Winter, waiting in the wings,
is not applauding Autumn's show.
Impatiently she waits her turn,
for lights to dim and colors go.

Then riding on her crystal sleigh,
drawn by the four winds, roaring loud,
she makes her entrance with aplomb
and lifts her hand to still the crowd.

She takes a breath as if to speak.
Her eyes flash with an icy stare
and all the world grows hushed as if
it were a goddess waiting there.

But when she speaks, her voice is bright,
like mountain torrents cool and clear,
cascading from some precipice
to unexpectedly appear.

The world awaits with bated breath
to see what she might next reveal.
Will she be cruel or kind this year?
How might she unleash pent-up zeal?

The four winds prance impatiently;
the crowd applauds and starts to rise
as winter gives her very best
and promises no harsh surprise.

Her face aglow with gentle light,
she waves her mittened hand yet higher
and sings of scenic days of ease
and cozy nights around a fire.

It Won't Be Long

A lily danced to life's refrain
through April rain
as robins played,
red throats displayed.

From branches high in cherry trees,
a lilting breeze
joined in the song ...
"It won't be long."

It won't be long till summer sings
and sunshine brings
her rainbow arc
to skies once dark.

Monterey Bay

Beneath the silver-surfaced sea
the strange, white-plumed anemone,
like mushrooms wearing dandelion puffs,
swaying in the tidal streams,
dance the silent dance of dreams.

Sardines in slick, tin-shiny skins
glide by in quick, bright schools, their fins
in rhythm with the ocean's gentle pulse.
Gray sting-rays flap their fleshy wings,
as far away, old Orca sings.

God's Symphony

I love to sit beside the ocean's shore,
and listen to its music rise and soar.
The melodic syncopation of its surging roll,
a numinous concerto without score.

What gift from heaven's bounty could there be
to equal earth's immense, majestic sea?
How grand the unseen hand that can arrange, control
this shining, ever-singing symphony!

Shadows

I thought I saw you yesterday.
I walked along a lonely path
where flowers bloomed and ocean spray
gave strutting gulls a cooling bath.

My mind flew back a dozen years
to when we'd walked this very shore
and planned a future without tears.
We shared a special, deep rapport.

You were the one assuring me,
if I would try, I could succeed.
You were the only one to see
how much my passion was my need.

I loved you so, and never saw
the rocky path you'd have to climb,
but suddenly, like coastal fog,
you disappeared before your time.

Life is, at best, a strange sojourn.
The tide sweeps in ... such joys we know!
But tides, like pathways, quickly turn
and take us where we would not go.

I love you still, my shadowed friend
somewhere beyond my longing reach.
Although you're gone, somehow you send
soft messages that guide and teach.

Prophecy

I hold a yellow daisy in my hand
and pluck the silken petals one by one,
while searching heart and mind to understand
how love so pure could slip to love undone.

Where once we walked in sunshine every day,
our voices raised in perfect harmony,
the world around us now has blurred to gray,
our dissonance expressed with stridency.

The petals at my feet remind my heart
that wholeness is much lovelier by far.
A flower, like a love, once torn apart,
cannot be mended. Is this where we are?

I dare not trust the petals' prophecy,
but hope instead, your love returns to me.

Wings of Hope

For every mountain there's a valley,
and for every sea, a shore.
For every daybreak, there is nightfall,
and a sky for every star.

For every desert lacking raindrops,
there are unseen hidden springs.
And so it is, where there is heartbreak,
hope glides in on silent wings.

Love's Perfect Boat

When life would toss us carelessly
upon it's tempest-ravaged sea,
there is one place it's safe to be ...
aboard Love's perfect boat.

It is the surest craft I know
to carry those who have to go
through stormy seas where cold winds blow,
and hope seems so remote.

Do not despair when doubts assail,
and you're caught reeling in the gale.
Love's perfect boat will never fail
to carry you with ease.

For Love, her mighty sails trimmed right,
will find a way through darkest night
and bring you safely to new light,
on morning's calmer seas.

Monterey Footprints

I miss the golden stretch of sand
that slopes from sea to street.
I miss the coolness of the waves
against my splashing feet.

I miss the smell of salt and fish
upon the cleansing breeze,
the seaweed strands that wash ashore
and curl like snakes with leaves.

I miss the joy of walking there
and watching seagulls soar,
their piercing cry accompanying
the breakers' crashing roar.

I miss the seals that hug the rocks
and flap their caudal fins
while drying in the warming rays,
bright sun on glistening skins.

I miss the playful otters too,
who float on velvet furs
and munch the crab between their paws,
then dive through drubbing surf.

But most of all I miss the joy
that filled each waking hour.
Those peaceful days refreshed my soul
like raindrops on a flower.

Cleansing Waves

I stood beside the rolling sea
and watched the rising swell
sweep from the sands the night's debris,
then wash the cliffs as well.

I thought … How like my Savior's love
which cleanses from my heart
the sins I am regretful of
and want to see depart.

For when I err, to my dismay
His heart is grieved awhile.
I'd so much rather live in ways
that earn my Father's smile.

Just as the rolling tides I see
sweep clean the sandy shore,
so shall His waves of love cleanse me
from sins I now deplore.

Where Light Abounds

Where light abounds, the meadows bloom
with fragrant blossoms. Soft perfume,
its scent abundant, fills the air,
intoxicating those who dare
to disavow their doubts and gloom.

They sealed the Savior in a tomb,
but brilliance filled his borrowed room.
There is no reason to despair,
where light abounds.

The Roman soldiers might assume
their plot had guaranteed his doom,
but suddenly he wasn't there!
Their prideful hearts were unaware,
all darkness is at last consumed,
where light abounds.

Silenced Songs

There is a grief as fathomless as sky,
which fills the heart and penetrates the soul.
It is a sadness not undone by tears,
but hovers like the clouds before a storm.

My heart is heavy with another's pain.
For such a grief, I find no remedy,
no words to ease the anguish of his heart
or fill the emptiness this loss has caused.

There is but one thing left for me to do.
I bow my head, and as the teardrops fall,
I ask the One who saw his own son die
and surely knows the pain of sorrow well,

to wrap my friend in comfort, much the way
a father holds a child whose loss he shares,
reminding him the darkest clouds hold light ...
the promise of refreshing rains to come.

I pray the rains of healing will begin
and cleanse away the brokenness and grief,
until, once more, his heart will fill with song,
and when it does, together we will sing.

Broken Wings

I was a bird, uncertain in my flight,
not knowing where to land or fold my wings,
but you, with grace and kindness, showed the way
as tallest branches reached to give me rest.

I was alone and cold, in darkness trembling,
the stormy night unlit by stars or moon.
But you, in kind compassion, gave me shelter
and taught me how to wait for light to come.

How can I then, when your heart aches with dread,
not offer you a soothing hand to hold,
or when you are uncertain where to turn,
how can I not lift high a lamp for you?

A friend is one whose heart beats next to yours,
whose hand is there to guide, though music fades.
A true friend loves through heartbreak or through fear
and offers hope when hope is hard to find.

When I was lost you never left my side.
When my heart broke, your caring halved the pain.
If yours is broken, I will carry you
until your own wings heal and you can soar.

A Prayer for You

I pray a prayer of intercession.
It's all that I can do.
Too distant for my intervention,
I'm glad God's there with you.
I'm trusting his strong arms will hold you,
keep you in his care,
and with his grace and love enfold you
as he hears my prayer.

Verbal Hug

If I could weave a blanket just for you
and send it in a box across the world,
I'd thread in strands of golden love so true
it would be dazzling when at last unfurled.

If I could bake a cake you'd like to eat,
I'd sweeten it with every sugared phrase
you've ever said to me … a massive treat …
one we could share together all our days.

If I could paint a watercolor scene
with all the rainbow colors you ignite,
and show the beauty I have found between
the lines of lyric poetry you write,

we'd have a masterpiece that could be hung
on palace walls, or in a gallery ...
But when I've finished this, I've just begun
to plumb the depths of all you mean to me.

So here's your blanket, here's your sugar cake,
and here's the masterpiece I've made for you.
Although it's only words, make no mistake …
the sentiments are real, these sayings true.

To Share Our Dreams

While very young, I looked for one
to share my dreams,
to rest with me when day is done
and starlight gleams ...
someone who'd listen with his heart
and hold me when the teardrops start,
who'd understand just what it means
to share my dreams.

It seems I found the perfect one.
We've shared our dreams
and proven life can be such fun!
We are a team.
Now that so many years have flown,
we face as one, the Great Unknown
with gratitude for what it means
to share our dreams.

Free Flight

Today I watched a seagull's flight,
and thrilled, enraptured by the sight,
as on the winds it seemed to play,
to soar and dip, then dart away on wings of white

as if it were a feathered kite
flown by a child, its string held tight
against the tug of winds which prey
on tethered toys that have no say about their flight.

More like the seagull's free delight,
is true love's course. No strings in sight,
love soars and dips and seems to play,
yet still returns at close of day, where hearts unite.

One Summer Day

All hearts cry out for love, and knowing this,
she went in search of love one summer day.
Impatient just to feel its breathless kiss,
she could not wait to give her heart away.

Her passion, warmer than the restless air
and stronger than the moon's relentless pull,
entreated her to cast off every care
and grasp what seemed to her so beautiful.

But what appears, in youthful innocence,
to be a gift too precious to refuse,
becomes, in light of gained experience,
a shadowed path most would not care to choose.

She chose the path that took her heart astray
and squandered precious gifts one summer day.

Passion's Flame

To linger close beside wild passion's flame,
is to assure in time, one will be burned.
Though carelessness or love may be to blame,
it matters not to one whose heart is spurned.

The leaping flames of passion which ignite
the thirsting soul of one un-watered tree,
can bring a sudden warmth, a glowing light
of joy that sets the tethered spirit free.

But when the flames die out and heat has flown,
the barren tree, with limbs to heaven posed,
remains a blackened shell, scarred and alone,
with inner core now ravaged and exposed.

Though passion's flame burns brightly at the start,
it is love's glowing coals that keep the heart.

Buoyant Love

Love can fill your heart with wonder,
like an island paradise ...
but can sometimes pull you under,
when the tides of discord rise.

If the waves of acrimony
wash upon your quiet shore,
or your loved one's sanctimony
leaves your spirit bruised and sore,

heed what sailors like to tell you ...
never fight a raging tide.
Trust the waves that will compel you
safely to the other side.

May your love be ever buoyant,
bravely sailing through the storms.
Whether days be sweet or poignant,
ride the crest as each wave forms.

A Quiet Force

Romantic ballads floating from the radio,
evoking tender thoughts that set my heart aglow;
a mountain lake so clear and blue my breath is caught;
an unexpected note from one I thought forgot --

a canyon deep and colorful, a waterfall,
an eagle soaring freely over treetops tall;
a tulip pushing up amid a mass of weeds,
or fields of golden poppies sprung from bird-dropped seeds --

the deeply heartfelt stirrings that a newborn brings,
these are the simple, yet profoundly moving things
which cause this poet's heart to lift a pen and write.
It is a quiet force I don't know how to fight.

A-mused

I write, not driven by a muse,
but possibly because I choose
to write; my purpose ... to amuse.

Amazed, I smile at the elation
brought about by such creation ...
words infused with strong sensation

then arranged in measured feet
while carefully, I count each beat ...
an age-old standard I must meet.

But, when at last my work is through,
and I've done all that I can do,
I hope my work amuses you.

I wonder, was it so with God?
Was He amused, while I am awed,
creating Adam out of sod?

And does it make Him smile to see
my meager creativity?
Might I amuse Divinity?

I write, not to amuse my muse,
but simply write because I choose
to be a writer, win or lose.

On A Sea of Silence

I floundered, lost upon the silent sea,
too far from shore to hear the sounds of home.
Westward, the sea stretched wide, a blue-green page
unmarked by any sight, save emptiness.

I longed for words to fill my lifeless sails
and carry my small craft to peopled shores.
But heaven held its breath and silence reigned,
except for silken tongues that lapped the bow,

their steady rhythm an iambic pulse
which seemed to sing a whispered song of love.
My hungry heart responded. Soon the breeze
began to move and fill the sails with life.

We soared like gulls across the rippling waves,
my craft and I, caught in the flow of words.
Though darkness fell before the journey's end,
the full moon lent her gift of haloed light.

In dawn's pale glow, we found the land we'd sought.
As waves cascaded up the sandy slope
and slipped away, receding foam revealed
my wind-wrought words strewn on the sand … a poem.

The Mystery

There is a wondrous mystery
that rides each cresting wave I see,
as breakers crash upon the sweeping shore.
I watch their surge from hour to hour
and long to know their mystic power ...
to lose myself within the ancient roar.

I wonder if there's room for me
within this roiling, churning sea,
or must I only marvel from afar?
And so it is with God, it seems.
He stirs my soul and lifts my dreams,
yet stays as enigmatic as a star.

Love Is Not Measured

Love is not measured in dozens of roses
or boxes of chocolates, or naming a star.
Love goes beyond all the questions fear poses
and gives, when to get would be simpler by far.

Love can be found when a heart isn't seeking
and sometimes when no one suspects it is there.
Love may be hidden in words someone's speaking
or wrapped in a hug that says simply, "I care."

Love is a banner, a shield and a shade,
protecting, restoring when all hope is lost.
Love remains true to the vows it has made
and never surrenders no matter the cost.

Love is not measured in tangible things.
It comes as a gift from the heart, freely given.
It need not be earned or deserved, yet it brings
the soul that it loves, a bit closer to heaven.

Roses are splendid, as are diamond rings,
but love is not measured in tangible things.

With Roses Nearby

The first time you kissed me, the roses nearby
released a sweet fragrance, an echoing sigh
that seemed to encircle us with a caress ...
a moment, a memory of pure happiness.

Our hearts were together that lovely fall night.
We whispered goodbye in the shadowy light
just inside the garden with roses nearby,
as the moon slipped away to the edge of the sky.

The sunlight of love shone so warmly that spring,
I was certain, without you, my heart could not sing.
So, though love was tender, we couldn't deny
we'd have to be married -- with roses nearby.

We vowed before God to be husband and wife.
You gave me a ring and I gave you my life.
But part of the promises you made to me --
wherever we lived, there our roses would be.

Like fragrant rose petals on winter winds blown,
the years of our lives have now gracefully flown,
but the longer we linger, the sweeter love grows,
like the delicate blossom of summer's last rose.

I hope you will know, when I take my last breath,
I've loved you through life, and will love you in death.
Our hearts are together as we say goodbye,
so lay me down gently, with roses nearby.

Stardust, Find Me

Serenely, starlight fills the evening sky,
Transforming trees and shadowed garden space,
Assuring me there is no need to cry ...
Reminding God is near, bestowing grace.

Despite the world and chaos all about,
Unbridled love now fills my heart with peace,
Suspending fear and driving out the doubt
Tormenters hope their evil deeds increase.

Forgetting darkness, I will watch the stars
Infuse the sky with heaven's holy light.
No earthly terror, nor the threat of wars,
Determines how my soul perceives the night.

Mendacity may reign a little while.
Eventually, Love conquers all that's vile.

The Wind Chimes' Song

Just as a midnight breeze awakens wind chimes' haunting song
to fill the night with music, so my heart sings along
with melodies remembered and memories unsung,
of moments sweet as honey on a hungering tongue.

Just as the summer sun returns to melt the mountain snows
that feed voracious rivers, my yearning heart now knows,
there is no sun so welcome as the sunlight of your smile,
to melt my frozen need and feed my aching soul a while.

Just as a thirsting flower lifts its greening leaves for dew
and drinks the gentle moisture, so my heart thirsts for you,
now trembling in its longing for your sustaining touch …
a warm caress to fill this place that misses you so much.

The Elusive Poet

I could compare him to a quiet lake
carved out of granite centuries ago,
its depths unfathomed, yet where warm springs flow,
while on its mystic surface, cool winds blow.

I could compare him to a summer sky
whose morning dawns with grey and crimson hues,
a palette only gifted artists use,
but who, at evening, writes with starlit blues.

I could compare him to a gentle lamb
whose purpose is to give ... I know not why.
His heart seems larger than a lake, a sky,
yet as elusive as a butterfly.

But in the end, no words of poetry
can quite define what he has meant to me.

Oh, How I Wish

Oh, how I wish I'd loved you more!
I cannot bear the sadness
of knowing when I had you here,
I squandered so much gladness.

Oh, how I wish you could have known
my heart's capacity.
Is it too much to hope you'll wait
inside eternity ...

and when, at last I leave earth's port
and sail to Heaven's shore,
will you be waiting, arms outstretched,
to hold me close once more?

Until that day, I know I'll grieve
for all that could have been.
Too late I learned to listen to
the love songs deep within.

Last Goodbye

Once more, beneath the old oak tree,
he smiled at me,
a shy half-grin,
then pulled me in.

His hug was strong and felt so right.
He held me tight
and let me cry
while time passed by.

At last I dried my tears. We knew
this was adieu.
I could not speak.
He kissed my cheek.

Waterfalls of Wonder

Waterfalls of wonder wash my mind
and form a rushing river through my heart.
Such wonders as I thought I'd never find
transport my searching soul to worlds apart.

I'm finding, as I make this rocky climb
where slipping is as certain as the day,
I have no fear of life's unwinding time,
for waterfalls of wonder mark my way.

The simplest forms of pleasure can evolve
into a fine surprise of wonderment.
A friend's warm smile, a touch that speaks of love,
cascade into a beautiful event

and tumble from the craggy cliffs around
to fill the pool below with life and power.
Like plants that burst with bloom from moistened ground,
my thirsting spirit thrives ... an opening flower.

The steps I take may not be easy ones,
and sometimes in the dark, I lose my way,
but still I find such overwhelming fun
in simple joys, like watching children play

beside the pool where tiny rainbows gleam
and bubbles dance as if they hear the song
of happiness that laughs within the stream,
to drown out troubling thoughts of what's gone wrong.

Some ask in awe, "Will wonders never cease?"
The answer lies within my waterfall,
as tumbling streams of happiness increase
and wrap my heart in comfort like a shawl.

Sonnet for the Children

I lie here in the dark imagining
there is another world beyond this night ...
a place where breezes dance and sparrows sing
and children play beneath sun's haloed light.

When just a child, such was the world I knew;
a life cocooned in love, untouched by fears.
With all my heart, I wish it could be true
for every child on earth who lives with tears.

Instead of pain and often senseless death,
I'd wish a life of joy, devoid of hate,
unmarred by guns that wound and stop the breath
and break the hearts of those who hope and wait.

It is my dream, may God's pure Child of Light
arise once more to fill this troubled night.

Sun-kissed Clouds

Though darkness hovers near the earth's horizon
and threatening storms are brewing in its midst,
faith teaches it is wise to keep your eyes on
the rim of light with which the clouds are kissed.

The glow reminds us God is always there,
although the clouds may seem to hide the sun.
There may be storms and burdens hard to bear,
but He makes all things right when day is done.

Gifts of the Morning

The sunlight drops from heaven like a sudden jolt
of hope into the very veins of doubt.
The chill of night soon vanishes as cheerful birds
announce among the branches with a shout --

A new day has begun! The weariness of night
must cease with hope's advent and light's onslaught.
I shove aside my weight of grief as if a quilt
and gaze with awe at beauty God has wrought.

There's nothing to be gained from weeping senseless tears.
I dry my eyes that I might better see
the marvels of God's world and all it signifies;
a world of wondrous possibility.

God did not sleep, but worked all through the starless night,
creating gifts of love He would bestow,
each one wrapped skillfully in wisdom's gilded words,
for children whom He loves more than we know.

I kneel to take my place before His holy throne
and there, receive the gifts prepared for me.
I've nothing much to give Him in return but love,
but this I humbly offer, gratefully.

A Spiritual Journey

For years I walked the well-worn paths
where many men have walked before,
through valleys green and shady-cool,
where flowers bloom beside a pool,
and laughing rivers pour.
There, fruit grows sweet on laden trees
and peace is whispered on the breeze.
My singing heart gave grateful praise
to Him who so enriched my days.

But then one day, while walking there,
I saw the sun slip past the hill.
The shadows filled the valley then,
and all the flowers folded in.
The air grew dank and chill.
I knew that soon it would be night,
but could not bear to lose the light,
and so, with tears and fearing still,
I left the path and climbed the hill.

But when I reached its windswept brow,
I stood amazed, and gazed in awe,
for far beyond, on every side,
the wondrous sunlit view stretched wide -
a vision without flaw.
The grace and wisdom of God's plan,
a splendor never dreamed by man.
My full heart sang out gratefully
to Him who showed such love to me.

The valley still lies green and sweet,
though shadows deepen and grow cool.
The fruit still beckons from the trees
and many men still walk with ease
the paths beside the pool.
But I will never walk again
the favored paths of other men,
for I have glimpsed a brighter way
beyond the hill - a whole new day!

The Waves of Time

The waves of time caress the shore
then slip away. They leave no trace.
Footprints we made are seen no more.
The waves of time caress the shore.

We came to wonder and explore
and leave a humble mark someplace.
The waves of time caress the shore
then slip away. They leave no trace.

One Christmas Night

One Christmas night I had a wondrous dream.
I walked in darkness through a snowy scene
and marveled that I did not lose my way,
nor was I cold, though why, I could not say.

I heard a bird whose song was like a bell,
a gentle chiming as the snowflakes fell,
and wondered if his singing kept him warm
or was it meant to sound a sweet alarm?

The snow fell thick and all grew strangely still.
The song, as if a symbol of goodwill,
continued through the cold and starless night,
but then grew silent in the morning light.

Remembering a child born long ago,
who came on wings of hope that He might show
the waiting world God's love and ceaseless care,
I wondered why I struggled with despair.

The message, like the singing of the bird,
resounded through the darkness, as I heard
what seemed to be a Father's tender call.
Oh, how I longed to understand it all!

I knelt and prayed the dream would never cease,
and that the child who came as Prince of Peace
would come again like sunlight in the sky
to dry the tears of all who mourn and cry.

When I awoke, I saw the sun was bright
and all the snowy world alive with light.
Just as I'd dreamed, a bird high in the tree,
began to sing a cheerful melody

that moved me strangely, filling me with song,
until I couldn't help but sing along.
"Oh Lord," I said, "All nature gives you praise.
I too would honor you in all my ways."

Though it was but a dream, my heart could feel
the transformation in my life was real,
and since that night, I've never been the same.
It was for me, the night the Savior came.

Ode to Mary

Young Mary, who had never known a man,
was startled by an angel one strange morn.
He spoke to her of an amazing plan –
a plan whereby God's son would soon be born.

Although she knew it would bring certain shame,
she humbly said, "Thy will be done in me."
As was foretold, the baby Jesus came,
and Mary loved him, knowing what must be.

As years slipped by, she watched her cherished son
amaze the scribes with his sagacious thoughts,
and marveled at the wisdom in this one
who was so much her child, and yet was not.

For he was God's and all the world's beside,
and knowing this, she saw him crucified.

In a Christmas Snow Globe

Small, silver flakes of whirling snow,
aglitter in my candle's glow,
surround a sweet and humble stable scene.
A mother rocks, with tender smile,
her manger-cradled baby, while
I feel as if I'm sharing in a dream.

A child myself, in silent snow,
I sense their joy, and somehow know
the magic of this special Christmas Day.
This precious gift which God has given,
wrapped up in love and sent from Heaven,
has made me want to give myself away.

The swirling flakes have settled down.
A peace descends on all around.
The radiant light of heaven fills the globe.
My candle flickers and expires,
but deep inside, God's holy fires
ignite the light of Jesus in my soul.

No Wonder

One night a brilliant star
lit up the eastern sky,
as in a stable far below
a babe began to cry.

He was too young to know
he too was Heaven's Light
sent from above into the world
God's gift of Love that night.

His mother sang a song,
as on a nearby hill
an angel choir also sang
while lambs and sheep stood still

and shepherds bowed in fear.
They could not understand
how this new babe in Bethlehem
was also God's pure Lamb.

But Mary held him close
and pondered in her heart
what God and all His angels knew ...
This was the humble start

of Jesus, God's own son ...
No wonder Mary sang.
No wonder stars lit up the sky
and angel anthems rang!

No wonder shepherds came
and knelt inside the stall,
amazed that they might meet this child
who would be King of all.

No wonder, even yet
we bow in reverent awe,
when entering the presence of
this One the shepherds saw.

To See Beyond

I gaze into the quiet waters of the lake,
its surface unruffled in the breezeless calm of morning.
The mountain sky reflects in the clear depths
and I watch the clouds, like wind-driven ships,
moving across its glassy surface.

I'm struck by the realization I need not always look up
to see what is happening in heavenly realms.
I have been given a perfect mirror here below.
How much more might I learn about the spirit world, I wonder,
if I were to gaze more deeply into the things of earth.

Just above the ridge of mountains,
the sun is rising as it always does,
blessing the world below with its life-giving rays,
and I think how much like God is this powerful light.

I feel its warmth on my shoulders, driving out the chill of night,
taking away the last remnants of darkness,
and my heart fills with gratitude to Him
who faithfully lights my way each day
and gives my spirit breath, as I bask in the warmth of His love.

I feel a gentle breeze begin to stir.
I can't see it, but I know it's there.
The surface of the lake ripples into delicate waves
beneath its feather touch.
I feel the brush of wind against my cheek
as it lifts my hair.

I'm reminded of His spirit
moving across a waiting heart,
lifting a soul to a higher place,
teaching us in ways we may not understand,
but the evidence is clear when He passes by.

The breeze moves through the trees along the shore
and the branches sway and sigh.
Birds take wing, calling out their greetings to the morning,
and I think of God's promise …
not a sparrow shall fall without His taking note.
I can't help but join my voice with theirs
in songs of grateful praise.

A New Robe

My earthly frame, my home a little longer,
is but a temporary resting place ...
a schoolhouse where life's lessons make me stronger,
equipped to meet the Master face to face.

At times I like to dream of that sweet morning
when I awake from silent sleep to see
His sacred head, with mercy's crown adorning,
arms opened wide in love, to welcome me.

Yet, I confess, it is a baffling dream,
for nothing in life's school can quite prepare
my soul to meet my Maker. It would seem
I'd need a robe of righteousness to wear.

But somewhere in God's Word, I found a line ...
He promises clean garments *will* be mine.

Nanna's Song

You bounced into my life one day,
and caught me by the heart.
I didn't know I'd feel this way,
or that such love could start

from kisses on a rosebud nose
or lights in soft blue eyes,
while feeling tiny fingers close
around my own. Surprise!

Your endless energy, your smile,
like unexpected sun,
have warmed my wintry heart awhile
and filled my life with fun.

Lovingly, you grace my world
with joy each time we meet.
I've never known a little girl
perpetually so sweet,

but you are this and so much more
than words can yet express.
To know you, child that I adore,
brings endless happiness!

Midnight Prayer

The moon, half full, beams on my sleepless face,
reminding me of God's unfailing grace.
Its light brings comfort to this darkened place
as prayer fills my heart for one I love.

"Lord, grant him peace and happiness," I pray,
"and let him feel your presence through the day.
If there is heartache, please take it away.
Surround him with a song like that above."

The moon sails higher in the midnight sky.
Its light casts shadows through the trees nearby.
As branches move beneath the wind's soft sigh,
I wonder what he might be dreaming of ...

I wonder if he'll feel my midnight prayer,
and, if he wakes to see the moon of there,
will he remember, these two things we share ...
moon's gentle light, and God's eternal love.

Love Must Let You Go

I sit beside your bed and search your eyes,
so strangely large within your fragile face.
I take your hand to feel its soft embrace
one moment more before your spirit flies,
and struggle with persistent hopes that rise,
seducing me to think this stricken place
is but a shadowed gate our Father's grace
will take us safely through. Then Truth replies,

This broken shell must now be set aside
that you might soar, a fledgling from its nest,
and on the warm, sweet winds of heaven, ride
to splendid heights of glory yet un-guessed.
To part with you is anguish I can't hide,
but love must let you go, to know God's best.

When Nights Grow Dim

The river of my tears flows without end,
as all that brought me joy flees from my sight,
for heaven bent to earth and took my friend
and left me here alone in sorrow's night.

Who will explain, or give a valid cause
for nights devoid of light ... no stars nor moon ...
a life in which the seasons seem to pause,
and bird songs hush as flowers wait to bloom?

But whether nights grow dim or seasons cease,
I am assured of God's unfailing grace.
He carries me in arms of strength and peace,
until I may behold Him face to face.

Then sun will shine, and flowers reappear,
as He who conquered death, dries every tear.

A Letter to My Fallen Love

Spring glowed in rows of daffodils,
and nearby lupin-painted hills
as well as in the luster of your eyes.
We heard the ocean's serenade ...
a love-song just for us that played
while we danced barefoot under sunlit skies.

Beside the surf, you held my hand.
I felt beneath my feet, cool sand
as, in your arms, we waltzed along the shore.
I watched the sunset's golden view,
while sheltered in the warmth of you,
and knew as each day passed, I loved you more.

We kissed beneath the moonlight's glow.
I felt emotion overflow,
when you, with tears, said you must leave tomorrow.
Your country needed you to fly
across the seas, perhaps to die.
I turned away to hide my own deep sorrow.

Spring fled, and summer too, then fall.
I waited for your weekly call,
those treasured moments listening to your voice
as tenderly, with mock concern,
you teased, attempting to discern
if someday I might make another choice.

I promised I would wait for you.
I knew no other love would do,
but then, with sudden fury, winter came.
Crisp, icy winds blew off the sea
the day they brought you back to me.
The love I lost can never be reclaimed.

The seasons circle endlessly.
I walk alone beside the sea
and dream of days long gone, when love was new.
The waves dance on the sunlit sand.
I long for you to hold my hand.
My broken heart cannot get over you.

Hiroshima

On star-tipped wings the giant eagle plows through
cloud-soft skies and finds its prey.
In streets below, feet pause on the pavement,
eyes turn upward, search, and know.
Voices cease. Hearts thump like drums.
Suddenly earth shudders and crumbles
in the heat of a thousand suns.

On the library shelves, books whose voices
once called out the wisdom of the ages,
now fall whispering, to ashes.
Glass panes at the windows
melt from their steel sashes
and flow like scalding tears
down the stony faces of the walls.
A man on the library steps leaves his silhouette
against the wall, and disappears.

The city, reshaped, stands stark in the mushroom shade.
At the shadow's edge, shimmers of light
shine from the blackened bodies
prone in the pale dust.

A ghostly silence floats in the empty streets.
Darkness precedes the night.
Far off, in the sun-lit distance, a great steel bird
screams its agony into the shattered skies
as God turns his face away and cries.

Footprints in Snow

A poet walked across my heart
and left his footprints there.
His silent shadow made me start,
as if my own despair

had closed the door to beauty's light
and left me in the dark ...
but still he came in love, despite
the coldness of my heart.

With heavy drapes soon opened wide
and shutters taken down,
the healing light of love inside
changed everything around.

A poet walked across my heart
and now, where once was sorrow,
melodic words of love impart
new hope for each tomorrow.

Someone Who Loves You

There's a bright, gilded moon hanging over the trees.
There's a Milky Way glowing with light.
There's a clear mountain lake in a warm evening breeze
and there's someone who loves you tonight.

There's a train clacking over the tracks far away,
and the low, haunting call of a dove.
There's a song on the radio you liked to play
for the someone who cherished your love.

There's a whisper of smoke from a summer campfire
and the fragrance of rain-dampened pine.
There's the tree-roses' bloom, like the scent of desire,
and the promise you gave to be mine.

Wherever you go, look around and you'll see ...
There's a moon or a song or a star.
You can never be free of reminders of me,
for my love will be there where you are.

After Sunset

There is a quiet after sunset,
when fading shadows in the trees
fold silently upon themselves
like worshipers on bended knees.

There, in the moments before darkness,
when the larks no longer sing,
but gather in the glow of twilight
to tuck small heads beneath a wing,

I search beyond the clouds, God's heaven
where first the evening star will shine,
and welcome it as if a promise ...
though darkness comes, His light is mine.

Just Before the Sun Goes Down

Just as the sun begins to set,
you take my hand and say,
"Let's have a quiet stroll, my love,
before the close of day."

You guide me out along the paths
of old Yosemite,
and as we walk, my heart fills up
with all you mean to me.

The path is rocky, like the road
that you and I have trod,
but you have never faltered in
your faithfulness to God.

His presence overwhelms me as
I view the river's flow
and contemplate the blessings that
are more than mind can know.

How rich my life with you has been!
You are my solid rock,
the one on whom I lean when I
can't find the strength to walk.

The years have bound us closer than
we ever dreamed could be
and love has grown as strong and tall
as any redwood tree.

I see the sunlight slip away
and know our walk must end,
but love endures and will sustain us
as we round the bend.

So, just before the sun goes down
upon our final years,
please hold me in your arms and kiss
away my happy tears.

Embraced

Embraced by love, I live in luxury.
There is no want your love does not fulfill.
When I awaken, you are close to me.
When we're apart, I feel your nearness still.

Your touch is kind, your words speak life and peace.
My heart rejoices at the thought of you.
I always know, though storms come, they will cease,
and after hurt, forgiveness will ensue.

But one day, we may have to recognize
this mortal life cannot go on much longer.
I see our slowing gaits, our wrinkled eyes ...
yet, though we fade, our love grows ever stronger.

Triumphantly, this road of life we've faced.
Whatever comes, by Love we are embraced.

Last Prayer

Release me from earth's binding tether.
Let me graze the plains of space
where love and mercy reign together.
Let me gaze on Wisdom's face.

Let my soul be free to wander
where no mortal can impede.
To the One all angels honor,
may the lights of heaven lead.

There, at last in His sweet presence,
let me bow in wondrous awe,
as the love that is His essence
cleanses from each earthly flaw.

In joy, my voice shall join that chorus,
singing of God's endless grace
which will, as eons stretch before us,
gather all in His embrace.

The Golden Door

There is a time when time will be no more
but we will not be sad because at last
we'll pass with joy through Heaven's golden door
and find our grandest dreams have been surpassed.

About the Author

Adonna Marie (Goodpasture) Gipe is a graduate of Point Loma Nazarene University, where she met and married her husband, Robert Gipe. After receiving a Bachelor of Arts, she began teaching in Yuma, Arizona, where Robert was employed as Office Manager with a large produce company.

Though she enjoyed teaching, she continued to pursue her love of writing, taking graduate and undergraduate classes throughout life, in poetry, article writing and publishing, and has devoted the last ten years primarily to writing.

Her hope in assembling these poems, was to provide a book that would not only be enjoyable for lovers of traditional poetry, but one that might also be useful for those who, like herself, love to inspire and teach other aspiring artists. The book contains samples of Shakespearean, Petrarchan, and Spenserian sonnets, blank verse, sonnet sequences, Villanelles, Rondeaus, Octograms, Rispettos, and many other forms a teacher of creative writing might use as illustrations in the classroom.

Adonna currently resides in Auburn, California, not far from her childhood home of Donner Lake, where she lived until graduation from high school. She believes life in that small mountain community contributed much to her creative inclinations. Her poetry often draws from the beauties of nature for inspiration and metaphor.

Endorsements

Songs Before Dawn, by Adonna Gipe, is perhaps one of the most aesthetically pleasing poetry books I have read in decades. *The poetry within this book blends a unique tapestry of poems of faith, love, contemplation, natural beauty and more. The poet skillfully blends deeply meaningful and beautiful phrasing to convey her thoughts. By this I once again refer to aesthetically pleasing poetry. Importantly, her poetry allows the reader to insert him-herself into the read, thus becoming part of the poem itself. Whether it's an English sonnet, quatrains, blank verse, etc., each poem within this book is stellar and leaves the reader sated, yet yearning for more of her verse. Without a doubt, Ms. Gipe's ability to create word art in the form of poetry is second to none.*

~ *Ray Griffin, teacher, poet, writer.*

Reflecting the heart of a true poet, Adonna Gipe has a masterful ability to weave words and phrases into beautiful, emotionally connected fabrics. Holistically, this inspired compilation reflects the comfort and freedom we find in literary structure. Most importantly, she reminds us of the security embedded in loving relationships, particularly with the One who guides us "and lends His hand to hold." (from Adonna's "The Path We Travel.")

~*Garrett Cooper*, former CEO of Ambassador Enterprises and Taylor University faculty member.

Songs Before Dawn is *an inspiring* collection that uses words as an art form. *It's a text book for teachers of writing, a gift for lovers of words, an inspiration to would-be writers and above all else, a treasure for aspiring lovers.*

~*Audrey Cole, former teacher*

Adonna Gipe has a lovely way with the right word. She cares that you see what she sees, feel what she feels, understand what she understands. She's a careful writer who works hard so her reader doesn't have to. Thank you, Adonna.

~ *Susan Rushton, Author, Creative Writing teacher, Columnist for the Auburn Journal*

CPSIA information can be obtained
at www.ICGtesting.com
Printed in the USA
LVOW12s1930011217
558305LV00015B/57/P

9 781458 221346